Praise for *The Coming China Wars*

"This is a well researched and illuminating book and is a necessary counter to a large body of opinion that posits an inevitable and even peaceful rise of China and chooses to ignore most of the author's message."

—Richard Fisher, Vice President,
International Assessment and Strategy Center

"What Al Gore does for climate change, Peter Navarro does for China. This book will hit you right between the eyes. A gargantuan wake-up call."

—Stuart L. Hart, S.C. Johnson Chair of Sustainable Global
Enterprise, Cornell University,
Author of *Capitalism at the Crossroads*

"A must read to be fully informed on U.S.-China trade. Hard nosed and impactful. Navarro lays it out."

—Peter Morici, Professor, Robert H. Smith
School of Business, University of Maryland

"Peter Navarro is that rarest and most valuable of China-watchers—an economist who sees the big strategic picture as well. *The Coming China Wars* contains the kind of realistic analysis needed by all Americans today, from voters to presidential candidates."

—Alan Tonelson, U.S. Business & Industrial Council

The Coming China Wars

The Coming China Wars

Where They Will Be Fought
and How They Can Be Won

Revised and Expanded Edition

PETER NAVARRO

Vice President, Publisher: Tim Moore
Associate Publisher and Director of Marketing: Amy Neidlinger
Executive Editor: Jim Boyd
Editorial Assistant: Pamela Boland
Development Editors: Russ Hall and Cynthia J. Smith
Digital Marketing Manager: Julie Phifer
Marketing Coordinator: Megan Colvin
Cover Designer: Chuti Prasertsith
Managing Editor: Gina Kanouse
Senior Project Editor: Kristy Hart
Copy Editor: Keith Cline
Proofreader: Jovana San Nicolas-Shirley
Senior Indexer: Cheryl Lenser
Compositor: Nonie Ratcliff
Manufacturing Buyer: Dan Uhrig

FT Press offers excellent discounts on this book when ordered in quantity for bulk purchases or special sales. For more information, please contact U.S. Corporate and Government Sales, 1-800-382-3419, corpsales@pearsontechgroup.com. For sales outside the U.S., please contact International Sales at international@pearson.com.

Company and product names mentioned herein are the trademarks or registered trademarks of their respective owners.

ISBN-10: 0-13-235982-0
ISBN-13: 978-0-13-235982-5

Pearson Education LTD.
Pearson Education Australia PTY, Limited.
Pearson Education Singapore, Pte. Ltd.
Pearson Education North Asia, Ltd.
Pearson Education Canada, Ltd.
Pearson Educatión de Mexico, S.A. de C.V.
Pearson Education—Japan
Pearson Education Malaysia, Pte. Ltd.

Library of Congress Cataloging-in-Publication Data

Navarro, Peter.

  The coming China wars : where they will be fought and how they can be won / Peter Navarro. — Rev. and expanded ed.

    p. cm.

  Includes index.

  ISBN 0-13-235982-0 (pbk. : alk. paper) 1. China—Foreign economic relations. 2. China—Foreign relations—Forecasting. 3. China—Commercial policy. 4. Globalization—Economic aspects—China. 5. China—Economic policy—2000- 6. China—Politics and government—2002- 7. International economic relations. I. Title.

  HF1604.N38 2008

  337.51—dc22

                          2007049932

To the memory of Darren Russell—a good son, a fine young man, and a very dedicated teacher.

Contents

Author's Comment on the Updated and Expanded Edition

Why go through all the trouble of writing an expanded and updated version of The World Is Flat *only a year after the book was first published? I can offer a very brief answer: because I could and because I must.*

—Tom Friedman

I offer this updated and expanded edition of *The Coming China Wars* because, like Tom Friedman, I can and I must. I can because, based on the initial success of the hardcover version of this book, my publisher thought it would be a great idea to offer a low-cost, paperback edition.

I must write Version 2.0 of *The Coming China Wars* for at least three reasons. The first relates to one of the lesser known, but more amusing quotations of John F. Kennedy. After a bruising campaign against Richard Nixon in the 1960 election, the new President would quip: "When we got into office, the thing that surprised me most was to find that things were just as bad as we've been saying they were."

My own surprise is not that the world's emerging "China Problem" is as bad as I said it was in the first edition. Rather, it is that many of the problems that I documented in that edition have become significantly worse—and have progressed much more rapidly than even I had projected. Indeed, since the initial publication of the book, not a day seems to go by without yet another chilling revelation about the dangers of a world economy increasingly "Made in China."

These revelations span the spectrum from exploding cell phone batteries, shredded tires, and fake Lipitor to poisonous toothpaste and deadly toys. But they also include startling news about broader global issues such as China's provocative blasting of a satellite out of the sky; its threats to "go nuclear" on American financial markets by dumping U.S. bonds and dollars; a rapid escalation in the harassment of foreign journalists; and China's continued and frankly despicable role in tragedies and events such as the Burmese repression, the ongoing genocide in Darfur, and a rogue Iran's destabilization of the Middle East.

The second reason why I must update and expand *The Coming China Wars* is that, based on a large mound of reader correspondence, I clearly missed coverage of a number of key issues. That's why I have added several new chapters to this edition.

One chapter absolutely essential for consumers and businesses operating in China deals in much greater detail with what has become an epidemic of contaminated and defective products from China. Consumers need to know how to protect themselves from this epidemic. Business executives likewise must learn how to ensure quality control when offshoring to the People's Republic—or risk costly recalls and debilitating lawsuits.

A second new chapter deals with China's very rapid Red Army buildup. Since publication of the first edition of this book, it has come to light that China's military budget is growing roughly twice as fast as its own red-hot economy. China's rapid and highly provocative military buildup includes modernization of what is already the world's largest standing army; construction of a deepwater navy to challenge the United States on the high seas; the addition of advanced nuclear submarines capable of striking U.S. cities with nuclear weapons; and a Chinese Air Force powered by the most advanced fighters and bombers available from the Russians. The political and strategic implications of China's arms buildup are worth a very close look, particularly because this buildup is quite literally being funded by the dollars that you and I spend every day on cheap Chinese goods in places such as Wal-Mart and Target.

A third new chapter very closely related to China's military adventures focuses on The Coming China Star Wars. While the U.S. space program continues its parabolic fade amidst budget cuts, embarrassing scandals, and interminable shuttle delays, China is aggressively moving forward with plans for a permanent Chinese space station, colonization of the moon, and travel to Mars. In conjunction with these bold plans, the Chinese are rapidly rolling out a massive space-related infrastructure that includes a powerful satellite network, a Global Positioning System (GPS) constellation known as *Beidou,* a fleet of deepwater space tracking ships, and ground stations established in Chinese client nations across the globe that will be capable of tracking U.S. military assets. The critical question examined in this chapter is whether China will be a friend or foe as it reaches for the stars; and you might find at least one possible answer to that question very disquieting.

A fourth new chapter squarely addresses China's human rights abuses, its suppression of free speech, China's brutal subjugation of Tibet, and what has become the world's biggest prison. Many readers questioned why I failed to address these topics in the first edition. As an economist, I originally thought these topics were more properly in the domain of politics. What changed my mind on this point have been several incidents involving self-censorship to gain access to the Chinese economy by three of the world's largest tech companies and Internet search engines: Google, Microsoft, and Yahoo! In the most despicable case, Yahoo! executives, hungry for business in China, played a key role in the jailing of a journalist who committed no other crime than forwarding an email message. Based on incidents such as these, it's clear to me that most of China's economic problems cannot be resolved without greater political transparency, and greater political transparency inevitably means the lifting of China's totalitarian curtain.

The third and final reason why I believe I must offer this updated and expanded version of *The Coming China Wars* is that I want to provide a much better set of answers to the core question raised by this book: How can we together fight and win these coming wars in a way that will benefit both China and the rest of the world? It is in this area of inquiry where critics found the most fault with the first edition.

For example, in his thoughtful review in the *Asia Times*, Benjamin Shobert wrote that *The Coming China Wars* "serves as an important touchstone for any prudent discussion regarding the implications to China's growth." However, Shobert also noted that the book "would have been more complete with an expanded emphasis on solutions to the issues he introduces." Echoing this theme, *Publishers Weekly* opined that "this informative book will teach readers to understand the dragon, just not how to vanquish it."

To firmly address this criticism, I have not only substantially expanded my own set of recommendations for consumers, workers, business executives, and government officials. I also offer sets of solutions that have been proposed by some of the most sophisticated China watchers in the world.

❖ ❖ ❖ ❖ ❖

I hope that you find this updated and expanded edition of *The Coming China Wars* to be a very useful tool to help you navigate through the increasingly rough seas of the twenty-first century. My primary goal in this book remains that of a "call to action." My fervent hope is that by raising the level of awareness about the world's growing China Problem, this awareness will translate into economic and political actions both within and outside of China that are long overdue.

Introduction to China's "Butterfly Effect on Steroids"

What happens in China, doesn't stay in China.
It's the "Butterfly Effect" on steroids.

—Ron Vara

Communist China has leaped onto the world stage as a capitalist superpower with astonishing speed. Today, China exports its vast array of wares at the competition-crushing "China Price," and we as consumers benefit greatly. If that were the end of the story, there would be no story—just an enchanting little ode to the virtues of competition in an increasingly "flat world."

Unfortunately, this story doesn't end with a cornucopia of cheap Chinese goods. Instead, this story about *The Coming China Wars* begins precisely at this point. It is a complex story about how the extremely rapid and often chaotic industrialization of the most populous country on the planet has put China on a collision course with the rest of the world.

At least one dimension of this complex story is already well understood. China's conquest of so many of the world's export markets has vaporized literally millions of manufacturing jobs and driven down wages from the heartland of America and the *maquiladoras* of Mexico to the slums of Bangladesh, the shores of Indonesia, and the once teeming textile factories of Africa. But that "good jobs gone bad" story, tragic and politically explosive though it may be, is only a very small piece of *The Coming China Wars* puzzle.

The *real* story provides a thousand variations on the famous Butterfly Effect of Chaos Theory in which butterflies flapping their wings in China set in motion a seemingly disparate and chaotic chain of meteorological events that eventually result in typhoons in Japan or hurricanes in the Gulf of Mexico. In this case, China is now flapping its mighty economic wings, thereby causing all sorts of energy, environmental, political, social, and military typhoons around the world. The myriad of dangers each of us now face from China's Butterfly Effects are very real and often quite personal, as illustrated in these fact-based vignettes from a "day in your life" in a world increasingly "Made in China":

- At the breakfast table, you turn on your Chinese-made TV to watch CNBC and watch intently as CNBC anchor Dylan Ratigan reports that another child has died from acute lead poisoning after swallowing a heart-shaped charm bearing the Reebok logo. The charm and its bracelet had been manufactured in China by a Reebok subcontractor that substituted cheap lead in the product to boost profit margins.

- Your spouse, one of the top-selling real estate brokers in your community, joins you at the breakfast table and promptly groans when CNBC economist Steve Liesman reports that interest rates and home foreclosures continue to rise in response to China's dumping of U.S. dollars in retaliation for a U.S. crackdown on defective Chinese products. Whereas you had the good sense to lock into a fixed-rate mortgage, your neighbor went the adjustable rate mortgage (ARM) route to save what he thought would be a few bucks on his monthly payment. Now, with interest rates spiking, his "exploding ARM" mortgage is doing just that, and he's maxing out his credit cards just to meet his payments.

- Later that morning, you walk out of Wal-Mart with a computer, a laser printer, a flat-panel monitor and some socks, shorts, and new running shoes. Outside, your eyes begin to sting, and your lungs begin to burn from the Asian "brown cloud" now visible on the horizon. It's 90-proof "Chinese chog"—a particularly toxic atmospheric smog that has hitchhiked on the jet stream all the way from China's industrial heartland where everything in your cart was manufactured.

- Driving home, you stop at a gas station to fill up your SUV at a very painful four bucks a gallon. As you watch the gas pump eat up your dollars faster than a Vegas slot machine, you listen to a report on your car radio about how China's addition of more than 100 million new cars to its highways and burgeoning oil demand have helped push oil prices over the $125 a barrel mark.

- Pulling out of the gas station back into traffic, you are horrified to see a sporty little compact car made in Shanghai scream through a red light and plow directly into a school bus when the car's counterfeit brake pads fail. Fortunately, none of the children are badly hurt, but the driver winds up in the morgue after the front end of his Made in China car crumples because of its low-quality steel and the driver-side airbag failing to deploy.

- That night, you get a very alarming call from the hospital. Your father has almost died from a heart attack because the Lipitor he bought at a local discount drugstore for his high cholesterol was a Chinese fake with no active ingredients.

Although each of these dangers is real, this book is not just a story about how China's emergence as the world's "factory floor" might personally affect you and your family. To illustrate the global reach of the China Butterfly Effect, consider these additional scenarios:

- A Filipino family of six is crushed to death when their newly constructed home collapses during a relatively mild typhoon.

Government officials later determine defective Chinese building materials are to blame for the building's failure.

- Ten American soldiers are killed in Iraq in a single week by armor-piercing Chinese bullets that slice through their body armor like a hot knife through butter. The bullets had been sold to the Iranian government by state-run Chinese companies as part of a much broader deal involving access to Iranian petroleum reserves. The bullets were smuggled into Iraq by covert Iranian operatives seeking to destabilize the Iraqi regime.

- Telecommunications are disrupted across Asia when a critical satellite is damaged by a large piece of space debris. This space debris was left behind when the Chinese military, without knowledge of the civilian government, blasted one of its own weather satellites out of the sky to test China's anti-satellite weapons capabilities.

- A severe drought hits South America, withering crops and driving up food prices. Climatologists blame the drought on the ongoing destruction of the rainmaking Amazon River Basin to make way for soybean cultivation. South America's soybean boom has been triggered in large part by dramatically increased demand from China, which continues to replace much of its own farmland with factories and industrial parks.

- More than 5,000 villagers in Darfur are forced to flee their homes after a coordinated attack by the Sudanese government that begins with a bombing raid by a squadron of Chinese-made Fantan fighter aircraft. This air assault is followed by a ground-based attack by Janjaweed militia—an Arab paramilitary force tacitly supported by the Sudanese government, whose goal is to completely exterminate black Africans in Darfur. In a classic "blood for oil" deal, the Chinese fighters have been sold to the Sudanese government—China's biggest oil supplier in Africa—in direct violation of a United Nations ban.

The purpose of each of these Butterfly Effect scenarios is to illustrate the incredibly broad scope of China's growing impact on the world. The purpose of this book is to warn that unless strong actions are taken now both by China and the rest of the world, *The Coming China Wars* are destined to be fought over everything from decent jobs, livable wages, and leading-edge technologies to strategic resources such as oil, copper, and steel, and eventually to our most basic of all needs—bread, water, and air.

Each of the next 11 chapters of this book focuses on one particular battleground. The concluding chapter is dedicated to finding constructive solutions to the emerging conflicts.

1

The Cheating "China Price" and Weapons of Mass Production

The China Price. These are the three scariest words in U.S. industry. Cut your price at least 30%, or lose your customers. Nearly every manufacturer is vulnerable—from furniture to networking gear. The result: A massive shift in economic power is underway.

—Business Week

The *China Price* refers to the fact that Chinese manufacturers can dramatically undercut competitor prices over a mind-boggling range of goods. As a result of the China Price, China produces more than 70% of the world's DVDs and toys; more than half of its bikes, cameras, shoes, and telephones; and more than a third of its air conditioners, color TVs, computer monitors, luggage, and microwave ovens. The country has also established dominant market positions in everything from autos, furniture, refrigerators, and washing machines to jeans and underwear (yes, boxers *and* briefs).

Given China's demonstrated ability to conquer one export market after another, the obvious question is this: What economic factors really drive the China Price? This is an extremely important question because the answer goes to the very heart of *The Coming China Wars* debate. If China is winning in the international trading arena on the basis of a cheap, well-disciplined labor force and superior manufacturing methods, that's one set of facts. It is quite another set of facts entirely if China is cheating, which it is. In fact, much of the China Price advantage is the result of slave-labor conditions coupled with a potent array of unfair trade practices that violate virtually every tenet and norm of international trade.

Cheap and Slave Labor—A Tough Combo to Beat

> *Yongkang, in prosperous Zhejiang Providence just south of Shanghai, is the hardware capital of China. Its 7,000 metalworking factories—all privately owned—make hinges, hubcaps, pots and pans, power drills, security doors, tool boxes, thermoses, electric razors, headphones, plugs, fans, and just about anything else with metallic innards.*

> *Yongkang, which means "eternal health" in Chinese, is also the dismemberment capital of China. At least once a day, someone is rushed to one of the dozen clinics that specialize in treating hand, arm, and finger injuries…. The reality, all over China, is that workplace casualties have become endemic.*

> *—New York Times*

Labor is undeniably cheap in China. However, wages are often lower in many other countries, such as the Dominican Republic and Nicaragua in Latin America, Bangladesh and Pakistan on the Indian subcontinent, and Burma, Cambodia, and Vietnam in Southeast Asia. Despite lower wages in these countries, none can compete effectively with Chinese manufacturers. Why is this so?

A major reason is that Chinese workers are better educated, more disciplined, and therefore *far more productive* than the typical workers found in the poor barrios of Managua or the slums of Chittagong.

In fact, after making the critical adjustment for their higher productivity, Chinese workers turn out to be more competitive than workers in nearly every other country in the world.

There is, however, a much more subtle aspect of China's cheap labor story—one that seeks to answer these two questions: How can Chinese manufacturers continue to pay such low wages for a high-quality work force in the face of rapid growth that would quickly tighten the labor market in other countries and cause wages to spike? Why do China's workers so meekly put up with some of the most dangerous and oppressive working conditions in the world?

The answers to these questions lie in one of great ironies of our time. In a country built on a foundation of Marxist-style communism, there exists in China the largest capitalist "reserve army of the unemployed" ever created. In this regard, one of the central tenets of Marxist theory is that capitalist exploitation of workers inevitably happens because capitalism always generates large masses of unemployment.

At least at this time in China's history, Karl Marx got it absolutely right. The size of China's reserve army of unemployed workers is breathtaking—numbering in the hundreds of millions. This reserve army of the unemployed is depressing wages for Chinese workers—and workers throughout the rest of the world. It is also allowing companies manufacturing in China—whether domestically run or foreign multinationals—to subject Chinese workers to some of the most repetitive, oppressive, dangerous, and truly unimaginable working conditions on the planet.

On the world's "factory floor," if the blades or presses do not sever a limb or take a Chinese worker's life, the dirt and dust in their lungs or the chemicals that seep in through their skin provide a much slower death. For those Chinese workers who do lose a limb or fall prey to a work-related disease, no functioning legal system exists to protect them. Upon being injured or maimed, they simply become the detritus of a ruthless manufacturing machine.

Beyond the Dickensian working conditions faced by the majority of Chinese workers, there is also the matter of slave labor—both real and contractual. Some of China's real slaves are the children, women, and occasionally men who are routinely kidnapped and forced to work in the brick kilns, coal mines, and countless sweatshops of the Chinese hinterlands with no payment other than a floor to sleep on, some rice gruel to eat, and the occasional beating for objecting to their enslavement.

Still other of China's real slaves are the millions of religious and political dissidents trapped in the Chinese equivalent of the old Soviet gulags. These prisoners of conscience are forced to work for nothing more than a crowded jail cell and meager rations. This passage from *American Legion Magazine* grimly describes the modern horror of China's primitive "laogai camps":

> After Mao Zedong established the People's Republic of China in 1949, he created a network of slave labor camps to maintain control over his subjects. The camps were called laogai based on a Chinese acronym for the phrase "reform through labor." Even though Mao died decades ago, the laogai camps remain an integral part of Beijing's tyranny.... Today, an estimated 4–6 million people are rotting away in the laogai camps, serving out varying years and degrees of involuntary penance to the state Mao erected. Laogai prisoners produce everything from bottled water and tea to electronics and engine parts. Given the religious reasons for many laogai sentences, it is a sickening irony that some camps even produce rosaries, Christmas lights, and toys—all for export to the West.

In addition to China's real slaves, there are millions more contractual slaves. These are the Chinese workers who arrive at the factory door wide-eyed and naïve, direct from the farms, expecting decent working conditions and a livable wage. In some cases, they are fed and housed, but their wages are withheld in a form of economic slavery. In other cases, these economic slaves may want to leave the job because the job has not lived up to their expectations. However, the penalties for leaving are so steep that they are stuck. To see what often confronts the typical Chinese worker seeking fortune in the big city, consider this excerpt from the *New York Times*:

> Each eyelash was assembled from 464 inch-long strands of human hair, delicately placed in a crisscross pattern on a thin strip of transparent glue. Completing a pair often took an hour. Even with 14-hour shifts, most girls could not produce enough for a modest bonus. "When we started to work, we realized there was no way to make money," said Ma Pinghui, 16. "They were trying to cheat us."
>
> She and her friend Wei Qi, also 16 and also a Chinese farm girl barely out of junior high school, had been lured here by a South Korean boss who said he was prepared to pay $120 a month, a princely sum for unskilled peasants, to make false eyelashes.... Two months later, bitter that the pay turned out to be much lower, exhausted by eye-straining and wrist-wrenching work, and too poor to pay the exit fee the boss demanded of anyone who wanted out, they decided to escape. But that was not easy. The metal doors of their third-floor factory were kept locked and its windows—all but one—were enclosed in iron cages.... Said Ms. Wei, "What they called a company was really a prison."

Of course, none of this ill treatment of Chinese workers could take place without the complicity of the Chinese government. This is a cold and callous government that imposes few health and safety regulations on its corporations and state-run enterprises. What lax rules do exist are only weakly enforced, evaded, or simply ignored.

The practical economic result of this dimension of the China Price is that the Chinese and multinational companies that grind up and spit out China's workers enjoy a very real cost advantage—and therefore unfair competitive advantage—over countries where workers have much better protections.

Lax Environmental Regulations—China's Rivers Run Black

The nadir of Zhang Jinhu's career occurred in the fall, when thousands of his ducks unsteadily wobbled out of the nearby river with singed feathers and burned feet, became paralyzed, and died. A prosperous farmer with a flock of 4000 birds here on the northern outskirts of Beijing, Mr. Zhang had weathered the sporadic deaths of some his ducks from caustic river water over the last few years. But he was not used to this sort of prolonged carnage. No one doubts the pollution in the sudsy green river killed the ducks. But in this relatively poor and extremely polluted country, there is often no simple remedy for the millions of people such as Mr. Zhang whose livelihoods have been destroyed by pollution. Though China has enacted strict antipollution laws in the last decade, enforcement is still lax in many places. Flagrant violations occur without so much as any serious investigation.

—New York Times

China's rapid economic growth has transformed China's once pastoral lands into the most polluted land mass in the world. China lays claim to having 16 of the world's 20 cities with the worst air quality. At the same time, as Dr. Elizabeth Economy documents in her elegiac *The River Runs Black*, almost the entire expanse of China's vast river system is severely polluted. In a macabre salute to its manufacturing hegemony, each year China's horrific pollution kills close to a million Chinese, while 20 million more fall ill to a variety of respiratory and other ailments.

Beyond this loss of life and human misery, there is this abiding fact of the China Price: All of those foreign and domestic companies operating in China that don't have to invest in expensive pollution control technology and that can indiscriminately dump whatever toxic pollutants they choose into China's air basins and rivers save considerable sums relative to competitors in other countries. That this, too, is an unfair trade advantage should be obvious.

More subtly, the biggest victims of this particular China Price driver may not be all of those workers who lose their jobs in countries around the world with much more responsible environmental regulations. Rather, the biggest victims of China's lax environmental regulations are the hundreds of millions of Chinese people who are forced to endure this endemic pollution.

China's "Nuclear" Option of Currency Manipulation

For the U.S. economy, it just might be the economic equivalent of a nuclear holocaust. China decides to dump the over $1 trillion in U.S. foreign reserves it holds—some 44 percent of the total U.S. national debt. The already-stumbling U.S. housing market is beaten into collapse. And the euro overtakes the dollar as the world's reserve currency of choice as America sinks into a deep recession.

It's not always easy to read the tea leaves in Beijing. But serious analysts say that in recent days, China has quietly threatened *that this* "nuclear option" *is very much on the table should the U.S. government attempt to force a revaluation of the yuan via trade sanctions.*

—Foreign Policy

China's next unfair trade practice to consider is one of its most blatant: *currency manipulation.* Because of this currency manipulation, the Chinese yuan is undervalued relative to the U.S. dollar by as much as 40% or more. This too-cheap yuan acts as a stiff tariff on U.S. exports even as it overstimulates U.S. consumption of Chinese exports. The result has been massive U.S. trade deficits with China that cannot be corrected in the normal, free-market way.

In the normal, free-market system of "floating exchange rates," large U.S. trade deficits with China would put downward pressure on the U.S. dollar and upward pressure on the Chinese yuan. As the U.S. dollar fell, the United States would sell more exports to China. As the Chinese yuan rose, U.S. consumers would buy fewer Chinese imports. These two free-market adjustment forces would bring U.S.-China trade back into balance while preserving U.S. jobs, particularly in U.S. export industries.

China does not, however, allow this free-market adjustment process to take place. Instead of allowing its currency to float, China pegs the value of the yuan to the dollar at a fixed rate, and China maintains this "fixed peg" by recycling U.S. dollars gained from its export trade back into the United States through the purchase of U.S. government bonds. In this way, China has become America's de facto "central banker," effectively financing both the U.S. budget and trade deficits through its currency manipulation as a means of creating jobs in China at the expense of U.S. companies and their workers.

China's role as America's de facto central banker is precisely why Chinese currency manipulation is so dangerous. Through the currency-manipulation process, China has accumulated over one *trillion* dollars worth of U.S. government bonds. Now, anytime that U.S. politicians threaten to penalize China for its unfair trading practices, China routinely retaliates with threats of its "financial nuclear option." Specifically, China threatens to destabilize the U.S. economy by dumping U.S. government bonds and dollars on world markets.

This is no idle threat. If China were to dump U.S. government bonds and dollars on world markets, it would cause the value of the dollar to plummet, interest and mortgage rates to soar, inflation to spike, the housing market to collapse, and world financial markets to plunge into chaos. That's precisely why even Chinese officials describe this dark side of currency manipulation as the "nuclear" equivalent of an attack on the U.S. financial system.

Some believe that China would never really drop its financial nuclear bombs because the Chinese economy would be hurt, too. However, the reality is that many top officials in the Chinese government believe that China is much more capable of withstanding such an economic shock than "soft Americans" used to the good life.

The Great Protectionist Walls of China

Under state control, many Chinese state-owned manufacturers are operating with the benefit of state-sponsored subsidies, including: rent, utilities, raw materials, transportation, and telecommunications services. That is not how we define a level playing field.

—Former U.S. Department of Commerce Secretary
Donald Evans

Any time U.S. politicians try to crack down on China's unfair trade practices, China and its growing band of Washington lobbyists quickly attack these politicians as "protectionists." A common tactic is to wave the bloody shirt of the disastrous Smoot-Hawley tariffs that helped cause the Great Depression.

In fact, it is perfectly reasonable for the United States to challenge China on its unfair trading practices. Indeed, the only real protectionist in this debate is China.

China's "Great Wall of Protectionism" features a complex web of direct and indirect subsidies together with an equally complex set of trade barriers that provide shelter to some of China's most vulnerable domestic industries and agricultural sectors. In the realm of subsidies, if you want to start a business, wouldn't it be nice if the government gave you cheap energy and water, free land, lavish research and development (R&D) grants, and whatever other capital you might need at bargain rates? Well, that's exactly what the Chinese government does for its export industries.

Of course, in the wake of China's entry into the World Trade Organization (WTO) in 2001, these subsidies and protectionist measures were supposed to melt away. However, China's compliance with both the letter and spirit of the WTO has turned out to be as big a farce and fiction as much of what appears in the heavily censored, state-controlled Chinese press. That's why around the world, more countries have lodged more antidumping and unfair trade complaints against China than any other nation! In this particular case, where there's smoke, there is a raging fire.

China's Buccaneer Corporate Edge

China is the epicenter of the counterfeits boom.... Just a few years ago, counterfeiting was all Gucci bags and fake perfume. Now it's everything. It has just exploded. It is many times larger a problem than it was only a few years ago. The counterfeit inventory ranges from cigarette lighters to automobiles to pharmaceutical fakes that can endanger a life. I would bet that there are companies that don't even know they're getting screwed around the world.

—Frank Vargo, National Association of Manufacturers

Chapter 2, "China's Counterfeit Economy and Not-So-Swashbuckling Pirates," describes in detail the immense scope of China's government-sanctioned counterfeiting and piracy. At this point, however, two points pertaining to the China Price advantage must be noted:

First, Chinese counterfeiting and piracy is an essential cost-cutting component of the China Price in at least three areas of manufacturing and production. Unlike U.S. automakers, pharmaceutical, and other R&D-intensive companies, their Chinese counterparts don't have to expend billions of dollars on research and development. Nor do Chinese companies have to spend millions more buying software and other IT components that they simply steal. Finally, Chinese pirates don't have to spend millions of dollars marketing brand names that they just rip off. Collectively, the money saved on R&D, software, and marketing adds up to a big cost advantage for Chinese manufacturers.

Second, the rampant piracy and counterfeiting that exists in modern China could not exist without the full support of the Chinese government. That's why no one should be fooled by the occasional and very highly publicized government crackdowns. The grimmer reality is that China tacitly supports widespread counterfeiting and piracy because such intellectual property theft creates tens of millions of jobs, helps keep domestic inflation rates low, and provides domestic consumers with purloined American, European, and Japanese products for pennies on the dollar.

China's New "Foreign (Direct Investment) Humiliation"

Companies are attracted to doing business in the People's Republic of China because of its low-tax development zones, cut-price abundant workforce, and totalitarianism. Independent trade unions are banned by the Communist Party. Assembly-line personnel in free-trade zones in south China operate machinery without safety guards and spray paint with inadequate face masks. They often die in industrial accidents or from gulaosi, *the Chinese term for death from overwork. Workplace death rates in China are at least 12 times those of Britain and 13 factory workers a day lose a finger or an arm in the boom city of Shenzhen. In a sign of official disquiet, the state-owned* China Daily *reported in November that*

a 30-year-old woman, He Chunmei, died from exhaustion
after working 24-hours non-stop at a handicraft factory....
Such miserable conditions allow China to undercut develop-
ing countries by up to 60 per cent.

—London Independent

The foreign direct investment (FDI) now flooding into China—close to $100 billion annually—is a critical component of the China Price advantage. Massive FDI is providing Chinese companies with two incredibly powerful catalysts for honing their competitive edge:

First, China's FDI is being spent on the most sophisticated and technically advanced manufacturing processes available. Such technology transfer means that China is getting much better equipment and machinery much sooner than other developing countries. This allows Chinese manufacturers to always produce more efficiently on the cutting edge and allows Chinese workers to experience rapid productivity gains that help offset any wage pressures.

Second, China's catalytic FDI has brought with it some of the best managerial talent and managerial "best practices" from around the world. The result has been a winning trifecta: cheap Chinese labor toiling on the production lines, local Chinese "scouts" who use their "guanxi" connections to grease the bureaucratic wheels, and the crème de la crème of foreign managerial talent in the middle and upper ranks.

One might argue that this aspect of the China Price is a perfectly legitimate competitive advantage untainted by China's other unfair trading practices. This argument is, however, dead wrong.

For starters, China's currency manipulation and its resultant grossly undervalued currency provide a huge and powerful magnet for FDI. This is because the undervalued yuan allows foreign multinationals to buy Chinese factories on the cheap.

Ultimately, however, one of the biggest FDI lures is China's extremely lax health, safety, and environmental standards. In what some critics rightly describe as China's second "foreign humiliation," these lax standards effectively allow corporations from Europe, Japan, South Korea, Taiwan, and the United States to export their pollution and worker safety risks to a country that has surprisingly few defenses against the vices of foreign capital. This passage from *Business Beijing,* which focuses solely on the role of China as a "pollution haven" for FDI, helps illustrate the broader problem of lax standards as an FDI magnet:

> Foreign investors have set up enterprises to decompose, renovate, and process waste metals, electronic appliances, tires, and harmful chemical pollutants. Most of them have a serious impact on the environment. Some of these investors even import foreign garbage into China, ostensibly for the purpose of recycling. Taiwan used to be an important location for recycling hazardous materials from the United States.... A number of Taiwanese investors have relocated their production facilities to the eastern mainland coastal areas of China, such as Shenzhen, Zhuhai, and Changzhou. They continue importing tons of waste materials such as used cells, vehicle plates, computers, adapters, and other electrical and electronic components for recycling in China. The effect on the surrounding environment is enormous.

The Cheating China Price Bottom Line

This foundation chapter is an important one because it exposes the critical relationship between *The Coming China Wars* and the unfair trade practices driving the China Price advantage. This relationship may be summed up by these four crucial observations:

1. *The Coming China Wars* described in this book are driven by China's rapid and unsustainable rate of economic growth, and China's hyper rate of growth is largely *export driven.*

2. China's ability to conquer export market after export market, often in blitzkrieg fashion, is made possible by an imposing set

of weapons of mass production embodied in the China Price advantage.

3. As we have seen, many of the China Price drivers constitute unfair trade practices that flagrantly violate both the spirit and letter of international law and trading agreements. These mercantilist trade practices include blatant currency manipulation, illegal export subsidies, lax environmental, health, and safety regulations, slave labor conditions, and a Great Wall of Protectionism.

4. To the extent that the foreign direct investment flooding into China is attracted by these unfair trade practices, this surfeit of FDI constitutes an unfair trade advantage, too.

❖   ❖   ❖   ❖   ❖

In the next ten chapters, we look at each of the major China Wars now being triggered by the cheating China Price and its weapons of mass production. The picture that will clearly emerge is that of a mercantilist country on economic steroids that has put itself on a collision course with the rest of the world. We shall also see why China increasingly faces a number of its own "wars from within" over everything from illegal land seizures, forced evictions, a crushing tax burden, and rampant government corruption to the transformation of China's once idyllic farm lands into polluted cancer factories, and the shredding of China's health-care system and social safety net.

2

China's Counterfeit Economy and Not-So-Swashbuckling Pirates

What springs to mind when you hear the words Louis Vuitton? But, of course, classic styling, tradition married to modernity, and the result—a unique, one of a kind Louis Vuitton handbag. You can buy a Louis Vuitton replica handbag for each day of the week for the price of one Louis Vuitton handbag. Apart from you and Basicreplica.com, no one else will know that your Louis Vuitton replica handbag was manufactured in China.

—Basicreplica.com

A lot of consumers may find it hard to feel sorry for big, fat cat corporations like Louis Vuitton or Disney when Chinese pirates and counterfeiters knock off their luxury handbags or first-run movies and then sell them for pennies on the dollar. There are, however, at least two big problems with this Robin Hood attitude.

First, Chinese counterfeiting and piracy are hardly limited to upscale baubles and Hollywood entertainment. Today, if America, Europe, or Japan are making it, China is faking it. Indeed, the list of counterfeit and pirated goods that China dumps on world markets quite literally runs the gamut from A to Z—from auto parts, batteries, condoms, and elevators to prescription drugs, semiconductors, shampoo, and even fake Zippo lighters that can explode in your face.

That's the second big reason why no one should take Chinese counterfeiting and piracy lightly. It exposes each and every one of us to quite often extreme health and safety risks. To understand the very real dangers, consider these fictional scenarios—which are *all* based on real-world events:

- Your scalp develops a severe rash because your knockoff "Head and Shoulders" shampoo from China contains toxic chemical residue.

- A small pebble shoots up from the tire of a truck in front of you and hits your windshield. The counterfeit Chinese "safety" glass does not crack but shatters, and shards of glass fly everywhere.

- Your prized Himalayan "lap cat" succumbs to liver failure because the tick medicine she was taking turned out to contain poison.

- In the dead of night, the counterfeit power strip that you bought in the bargain bin of the local hardware store starts an electrical fire. Your smoke detector does not work because your fake "Duracell" batteries leaked acid all over the alarm system. Did you get out of the house before it burned down?

- Your brother orders what turns out to be fake Viagra over the Internet because he is too embarrassed to ask his doctor for a regular prescription. After a nice candlelight dinner with his spouse, he winds up in a hospital bed with a wild heartbeat. The very next week, your mother winds up in the same hospital with a broken hip because her phony "Evista" medication for osteoporosis was nothing more than molded chalk.

- On a sultry summer night, two of your co-workers—a 22-year old gay man and a 24-year old heterosexual woman—buy fake "Durex Extra Safe" condoms at the same pharmacy. Later that night, in separate encounters, the condoms burst. The gay man gets HIV, and the woman contracts chlamydia, which renders her sterile.

China's Counterfeit Kings and Grand Theft Auto

It's a busy September afternoon at the Zhiyou Automotive Parts Market in this southern port city [of Guangzhou, China]. Messengers zoom in and out of the square on motorcycles carrying orders. Vans pull up to load and unload. Buyers and vendors haggle over prices at stalls that display parts from every single major automaker and parts maker in the world. Fram filters. Ford accessories. Champion spark plugs. Philips and Bose audio systems. BMW wheels. All at discount prices and all in their original packaging. But most, if not all, are fake.

—*Automotive News*

Piracy refers to the unauthorized production, distribution, or use of a good or service. The goal of a pirate is to create a look-alike knockoff that can be sold to a customer as a knockoff, not passed off as the real thing.

Counterfeiting ups the piracy ante by pawning off pirated products as that of the real, branding corporation. Thus, a golf club that looks just like a Callaway driver but has a name like "Hallaway" is a pirated knockoff, whereas a knockoff sold as a Callaway club is a counterfeit. The World Customs Organization estimates that such counterfeit and pirate activities represent close to 10% of all world trade!

Of course, China is not the only pirate nation. Other hotbeds include Russia, India, Vietnam, South Africa, and even tiny Paraguay on the notorious Triple Frontier region bordering Argentina and Brazil.

China is, however, hands down, the biggest buccaneer on the planet—with its *de facto* nationalist banner no longer Mao's five-star red flag but the infamous Jolly Roger. The statistics speak loudly and clearly for themselves: China accounts for two-thirds of all the world's pirated and counterfeited goods and fully 80% of all counterfeit goods seized at U.S. borders. The long list of purloined products includes consumables such as baby food, soft drinks, and hard liquor and common household products such as makeup, perfume, and razors. It likewise encompasses big-ticket items such as air conditioners and refrigerators. It extends even to the lofty elevator and the lowly toilet seat.

China's pirate producers and counterfeiters come in many shapes and sizes and under many guises and disguises. Here is one typical "ghost-shift" scenario of how such piracy occurs in what has become a global supply chain of piracy and counterfeiting: A factory in China is hired by an American company to make 1,000 units of a product per day. However, rather than just run two regular 8-hour shifts to produce the contracted-for amounts, the factory also runs a third "ghost shift," and then ships the extra 500 items a day out the back door.

Another variation on this theme is China's ubiquitous use of "reverse engineering," which involves taking machines or products apart to figure out how to copy them. Through reverse engineering, Chinese counterfeiters have been able to get knockoffs of everything from Suzuki motorcycles to Callaway golf clubs on the street just weeks after these new products have been introduced to the market.

One of the most lucrative—and dangerous—counterfeit sectors in China is cigarettes. Rivaling any one of the big multinational producers, China churns out 65% of the world's counterfeit sticks. Of the more than 35 billion cigarettes it produces annually, almost 30 billion are exported.

Cigarette counterfeiting is largely a clandestine cottage industry, as many of China's small cigarette production facilities are quite literally underground, either in basements or in subterranean rooms accessible only by tunnels. As James Nurton has noted, in these hidden dens "counterfeiters will hire workers for just a few days or even hours to produce a batch of counterfeit cigarettes using old machines and hand-rolling the finished product." In such clandestine environs, cigarettes, already one of the most efficient killers of the human species, often become even more deadly. Indeed, those counterfeit Marlboros or Camels for the macho male set or those fake Virginia Slims for the ladies may contain five times as much cadmium as genuine cigarettes, six times as much lead, and high levels of poisonous arsenic.

As a smuggling strategy, the cigarettes are often exported along with, and within, packets of tea. Because tea and tobacco weigh roughly the same, the contraband is difficult to detect. Moreover, the profit margins are astronomical. Notes Nurton, "with the typical cost of a container just $120,000, counterfeiters can make millions of dollars of profit on just one shipment."

An equally lucrative sector of China's knockoff economy is that of replacement auto parts. Chinese pirates account for 70% of all counterfeit auto parts in the world, and, as a clear red flag to any prospective consumer, more than half of all Chinese vehicles contain counterfeit components.

In contrast to the highly decentralized cigarette counterfeiting operations, auto part piracy is supremely well-organized. Fake products include everything from brake pads, oil filters, and fan belts to fenders, engine blocks, windshields, and windshield wipers. Given that selling new cars is often a "loss leader" to establish a lucrative aftermarket in replacement parts, such counterfeiting represents a particularly crippling form of economic "cream skimming" that cuts deeply into the bottom line of the legitimate auto industry. As *Forbes* notes: "Replacement parts are to car companies what popcorn is to movie theaters. It's how they pay the rent."

There are also significant safety issues for an industry in which several tons of metal traveling at high speeds depend on equipment reliability. In some cases, the quality and appearance of the fake auto parts is so good that is difficult to distinguish between a fake and an original product. In many other cases, the parts are of such poor quality that they are doomed to early and often-dangerous failure. As reported in *Automotive News,* some of the "many horror stories" include "brake linings made of compressed grass, sawdust or cardboard; transmission fluid made of cheap oil that is dyed; and oil filters that use rags for the filter element."

The dangers (and company liabilities!) inherent in the fake auto parts market have been rhetorically noted by an executive from the heavy-duty truck industry: "How would you like to have fake brakes with your brand name on them installed on a heavy truck, which happens to be bearing down on a stalled school bus?"

It is not just auto parts that China's pirates steal in this industry. In a mushrooming problem, Chinese manufacturers have taken to ripping off entire vehicle designs across the manufacturing spectrum.

In today's not-so-swashbuckling China, the compact SUV Honda CR-V is being faithlessly replicated by China's Laibao S-RV. Toyota's land cruiser Prado SUV has been cloned as the Dadi Shuttle. The luxury Mercedes C-Class has been reincarnated as the Geely Meerie. The Rolls-Royce Phantom has a bastard twin in the Hongqi HQD. Even luxury buses are not immune, with Neoplan's Starliner now carbon copied as the Zonda A9. In what might be darkly comical under other circumstances, China is also producing a variety of "Frankenstein cars" that feature the front end of one car, the back end of another, and still other features from other cars.

As with China's purloined auto parts, China's grand theft auto is not only outrageous. It is also a tragedy waiting to happen. Although each pirated vehicle may look like the real thing, most are deathtraps on wheels (put together with inferior metals, materials, and an array of counterfeit parts) and, as detailed in the next chapter, consistently perform miserably in crash tests.

China's Snake Oil for the World

In January, Honor International Pharmtech was accused of shipping counterfeit drugs into the United States. Even so, the Chinese chemical company—whose motto is "Thinking Much of Honor"—was openly marketing its products in October to thousands of buyers here at the world's biggest trade show for pharmaceutical ingredients.

Other Chinese chemical companies made the journey to the annual show as well, including one manufacturer recently accused by American authorities of supplying steroids to illegal underground labs and another whose representative was arrested at the 2006 trade show for patent violations. Also attending were two exporters owned by China's government that had sold poison mislabeled as a drug ingredient, which killed nearly 200 people and injured countless others in Haiti and in Panama.

Yet another chemical company, Orient Pacific International, reserved an exhibition booth in Milan, but its owner, Kevin Xu, could not attend. He was in a Houston jail on charges of selling counterfeit medicine for schizophrenia, prostate cancer, blood clots, and Alzheimer's disease, among other maladies.

—New York Times

Until recently, Marilyn Arons' only experience of counterfeit goods was the fake Louis Vuitton handbag she bought on the street…. When she learned in March that her refill of Lipitor, a popular cholesterol-lowering drug, contained fake pills, she had plenty of angry, anxious thoughts on the matter. "If it wasn't Lipitor I was taking," she worried, "what was it?" Arons, who is suing several drug distributors, says she was furious when her pharmacist told her she would be fine. "Would you be fine," she demanded, "if I paid you with counterfeit money?"

—U.S. News & World Report

As Lembit Rägo of the World Health Organization has succinctly put it: "Counterfeit drugs kill people." Make no mistake about it, the risks are high. Today, at least one out of every ten containers of medicine worldwide is fake.

To understand the dangers, consider this small sample of drugs from China's counterfeit pharmaceutical factories: cough syrup laced with antifreeze; meningitis vaccine and anemia drugs made from tap water; birth control pills that are nothing but compressed wheat flour, Lipitor and Norvasc for high cholesterol and high blood pressure without any active ingredients; Viagra and Cialis laced with strychnine; and malaria pills without a trace of their critical ingredient (*artusenate*).

China's dominant role in the counterfeit drug trade is not just because of a huge production capacity and sophisticated distribution network. It is also because as fast as you can say, "Can you fill this prescription, please?" China's highly skilled pirates are able to reproduce the so-called blister packaging, vacuum-formed clamshells, fake holograms, and distinctive pills so artfully and faithfully that drug companies typically can only detect fakes by using complex lab testing. This counterfeiting capability is no small feat, particularly since pharmaceutical companies continue to boost the complexity of their packaging in an effort to thwart counterfeiting.

The uncanny ability of the Chinese to excel in highly sophisticated piracy is attributable to precisely the same factors that have allowed China to become the world's factory floor. Chief among them is the flood of *foreign direct investment* that has brought in all the latest sophisticated machinery necessary to knock off whatever drug or product from which money can be made. When the pills and packaging are complete, China's counterfeit drug dealers then harness many of the same transportation, distribution, and sales channels established for legitimate purposes by foreign companies in China to distribute the illegitimate products worldwide.

Nor does it necessarily take a huge factory to produce counterfeit drugs. One of the simplest ways to create a phony batch of Viagra is to start with some of the authentic pills. Grind these up, add a little bulking agent such as boric acid, and remold the pills. Presto! You now have Chinese-style "Viagra Lite." Oh, and by the way, boric acid's more common use is as a pesticide to kill cockroaches and termites by attacking their nervous systems.

Whether it's counterfeit Lipitor, Norvasc, Viagra, or Tamiflu, fake Chinese drugs can find their way into your medicine cabinet in many ways. In some cases, it happens when a big chain such as Rite Aid gets fooled by a supplier. In other cases, it happens when a small local pharmacy tries to keep its costs down by buying odd lots from wholesalers. More often than not, however, it is the increasingly double-edged sword called the World Wide Web that delivers these deadly drugs from the bowels of eastern China to people's doorsteps. Consider these typical profiles of Internet drug consumers, who become all-too-easy prey for China's drug pirates:

- A Social Security couple who are already being eaten alive by medical expenses needs a new drug not yet covered by insurance or Medicare. So, they try an online "Canadian" pharmacy that offers cheap drugs but that is really operating out of Heilongjiang Province in Northeast China.
- A housewife suffering from chronic depression is too embarrassed to go to the local pharmacy for her Prozac so she opts for the anonymity of the Internet, while her workaholic, jet-traveling husband is simply too busy to get his Ambien sleeping pills anywhere else. Meanwhile, their weightlifting 17-year-old son has been secretly going online for his monthly orders of muscle-popping Deca-Durobolin anabolic steroids.
- Finally, and as the anchor of the Internet boom in counterfeit drugs, there is the aging Baby Boomer who is not as good as he once was in the bedroom but wants to be as good once as he ever was. He is the easiest mark of all for the pirates and the number one reason why Viagra is the Internet's top-selling counterfeit drug.

Chinese Piracy Economics 101

The handbag has a much better mark-up than heroin.

—Andrew Oberfelt, Abacus Security

Why has China emerged as the world's pirate king? The simplest answer is that at least in this case, crime pays—and the payoffs are huge.

A major reason why counterfeiting and piracy is so profitable is that China's rip-off artists do not have to engage in research and development to produce a product or design. They just steal the intellectual property after it is produced. That saves enormous sums, particularly in R&D-intensive industries such as automaking and pharmaceuticals.

China's pirates also do not have to spend huge sums of money on advertising and marketing to build and sustain a brand name and open new markets. They just piggyback on the efforts of legitimate companies—while in the process, destroying much of the brand value and goodwill that a company builds up at huge expense.

Perhaps most interestingly, Chinese counterfeiters and pirates are every bit as good at achieving high production efficiencies as any large, modern multinational corporation. As noted in the *Chinese Business Review,* "A smart counterfeiter is likely to produce fakes of several companies' products in a particular product line." Moreover, "this duplication occurs in many product lines, whether software, film, batteries, or auto parts." The ability of Chinese counterfeiters pirates to use production facilities to churn out multiple but related products in large volumes is the very definition of economies of scope and scale and allows these intellectual property thieves to produce at substantially lower unit costs. For all these reasons, China's counterfeiters and pirates have a huge cost advantage over legitimate producers.

A final element of Piracy Economics 101 speaks to the increasingly important role that organized crime plays in pirate activity. With a sophistication rivaling any MBA-trained top executive corps, China's crime networks are now diverting resources out of traditional gang staples such as drugs and prostitution and into counterfeiting on the basis of pure economics. As Oded Shenkar has noted: Whereas a drug dealer might double his money on a kilo of heroin, that same dealer "can buy 1,500 pirated copies of Microsoft Office and pocket a 900 percent profit." Moreover, if a Chinese gang member is caught peddling heroin or speed, it's ten years or more in the slammer, depending on the country. But if he is caught peddling something far more deadly—impotent Lipitor or heart-stopping Viagra—it is a small fine and slap on the wrist.

Chinese Piracy Politics 101

No problem of this size and scope could exist without the direct or indirect involvement of the state.

—Professor Daniel C. K. Chow, Ohio State University

All of our observations thus far about the favorable economics of Chinese counterfeiting and piracy still do not explain why, despite an occasional highly publicized crackdown, the Chinese government tacitly supports these illegal activities. The reason goes back to both basic economics and politics—with a particular Chinese cultural twist.

With counterfeiting and pirate activities contributing as much as 20% or more of China's economic growth, state-sanctioned piracy and counterfeiting is a vital component of government policy. This intellectual property theft creates millions of jobs, helps control inflation, and raises the standard of living for many of the Chinese people. As anti-counterfeiting expert Li Guorong has noted, "Counterfeiting is now so huge in China that radical action would crash the economy overnight [and] even destabilize a government where counterfeit factories and warehouses are often owned by local military and political grandees."

These economic and political motives for Chinese piracy are strongly reinforced by a set of cultural norms that flow from an amoral fusion of a 60-year old Maoism and a centuries-old Confucianism. The core problem is that the government of the People's Republic of China was founded in 1949 on the abolition of private property. Thus, there exists several generations of Chinese executives who truly believe that, as former U.S. ambassador James Lilley has noted, "Any technology in the world is the property of the masses."

When one adds to this Maoist version of property rights a large dose of Confucianism, the counterfeiting and piracy picture comes much more sharply into focus. Since ancient times, Confucianism has revered, rather than reviled, imitation. The result is the perfect economic, political, and cultural laboratory for a counterfeiting and piracy boom. *Caveat emptor!*

3

"Made in China"—The Ultimate Warning Label

A mother said Thursday she knew something was terribly wrong when her 20-month-old son began to stumble and started vomiting. He had just ingested Aqua Dots, a popular toy that contains a chemical that turns into a powerful "date rape" drug when eaten. It was the latest Chinese-made toy pulled from shelves in North America.

—MSNBC.com

"Beware of cheap Chinese goods that can kill you." If that little Confucian warning doesn't appear in your next fortune cookie, it should. As Upton Sinclair spins in his grave, China is flooding the world with a staggering array of cancerous, contaminated, and defective products.

No doubt you have already heard about some of the worst cases. In the toxic metals category alone, we've seen baby cribs, vinyl bibs, and children's gardening gloves lined with lead; toy bears, drums, and trains coated with lead paint; lead snaps on Chinese-made overalls and shirts for babies and toddlers; and a complete line of Barbie doll accessories decked out in "designer lead."

You have also likely heard about the cough syrup and toothpaste laced with antifreeze that killed hundreds of people; the pajamas soaked in so much formaldehyde they make your skin crawl; the cat and dog treats spiked with deadly melamine that prematurely put tens of thousands of Garfields and man's best friends into pet cemeteries; and, as the hands-down winner of the most bizarre form of Chinese product torture, "Aqua Dots"—the toy beads *cum* date rape drug featured in the excerpt opening this chapter.

Sensational though these headline grabbers may be, they are but the tip of a very dangerous iceberg. From exploding cell phone batteries, bacteria-ridden tofu, and catfish loaded to the gills with banned antibiotics to cheap Chinese cars so dangerous they make crash dummies run for cover, virtually nothing coming out of today's China should be considered safe. This chapter shows you just why this is so, just what kind of products you should fear most, and why, as Senator Dick Durbin has aptly noted, "Made in China" has become a code red "warning label" that no sensible consumer should ignore.

A Poisoned Food Chain

You've got to be nuts to eat Chinese food.

—Ron Vara

Most people quite rightly think of China as a manufacturing powerhouse and the world's "factory floor." Increasingly, China is also becoming the world's fish farm, fruit orchard, and vegetable garden.

Today, China is the third largest exporter of food to the United States. China accounts for more than 50% of the garlic, 45% of the apple juice, roughly 20% of the honey, and about 15% of the seafood imported into the United States. Incredibly, the U.S. Food and Drug Administration (FDA) tests less than 1% of all food imports into the U.S. This is in sharp contrast to Japan, which tests fully 10%. As noted in *USA Today,* this understaffing of the FDA "signals a large green light for produce and seafood to enter the U.S. market without having to sweat inspections."

Something So Very Fishy

Perched above the banks of the catfish farm he owns is Zhu Zhiqiu's secret weapon for breeding healthy fish: the medicine shed. Inside are iodine bottles, vitamin packets, and Chinese herbal concoctions that he claims substitute for antibiotics. Zhu's fish farm, in a village on the lower reaches of the Yangtze River, sends about 2.5 million catfish fillets each year to United States through an importer in Virginia. Despite his best efforts—he has dozens of employees clearing trash from the water each day, and the fish are fed sacks of fishmeal more expensive than rice—Zhu's fish sometimes get sick. Then he brings out the drugs.

—*Washington Post*

China is the leading exporter of catfish, eel, and tilapia to the United States and the second biggest shrimp supplier. China is also the world's leading exporter of toxic seafood.

The problem of toxic fish begins with the observation that Chinese fish farmers, like Mr. Zhu in the preceding excerpt, inevitably are forced to rely on a dizzying array of banned antibiotics, herbal concoctions, and illegal substances to get their fish to market. The underlying problem, discussed extensively in Chapter 7, "The Damnable Dam and Water Wars—Nary a (Clean) Drop to Drink," is that the waterways of China are some of the most severely polluted in the world and therefore some of the least habitable for fish. In such a polluted environment, farm-bred fish are particularly vulnerable to the big four pathogens: viruses, bacteria, fungi, and parasites.

One common way China's fish farmers cope with two of these pathogens—fungi and external parasites—is to douse the waters of their farms with a powder known as *malachite green*. This strong green dye is a dangerous carcinogen that has been officially banned in China. However, that ban hasn't stopped many of China's fish farmers from using it.

A second common way China's fish farmers keep their fish from dying is to flood the waters with a variety of banned antimicrobials and antibiotics. The antimicrobials are known carcinogens that can kill you directly. In contrast, the banned antibiotics can kill or harm you indirectly. The reason is a subtle one: When you eat fish laced with antibiotics, you can build up a resistance to these drugs. Then, if you get sick and actually need the antibiotics to fight the infection, the antibiotics simply won't work. In addition, the bacteria can evolve into "superbugs" highly resistant to the antibiotics.

In addition to having to worry about all manner of toxins creeping into Chinese fish, consumers around the world have to contend with China's "fish counterfeiters." For example, one common ploy used by unscrupulous Chinese exporters is to sell the dangerous puffer fish disguised as the delectable monkfish. The problem here is that puffer fish contain tetrodotoxin. This is a potent neurotoxin for which there is no known antidote; it produces paralysis of the diaphragm and often death due to respiratory failure.

Midnight in China's Fruit and Vegetable Gardens of Evil

For nearly two decades, Lai Mandai regularly ate and sold beans, cabbage, and watermelons grown on a plot of land a short walk from a lead smelting plant in her village. Like dozens of other villagers who ate locally grown food, Ms. Lai, 39 years old, developed health problems. "When I did work, planting vegetables or cleaning the floor, I felt so tired and my fingers felt numb," Ms.Lai says. Ms. Lai, along with 57 other villagers, was eventually diagnosed with high levels of cadmium, a heavy metal that can cause kidney disease and softening of the bones.

—Wall Street Journal

China grows half of the world's vegetables and almost 20% of its fruit. China's people consume most of its produce, but an increasing share is being exported to the United States, Europe, and the rest of the world. As with China's toxic fish exports, this is not an altogether welcome development.

One of the biggest problems with eating Chinese fruit and vegetables is the rising risk of ingesting one of any number of highly toxic heavy metals, including mercury, lead, and the cadmium that felled Ms. Lai in the preceding excerpt. In fact, according to China's own Ministry of Land and Resources, more than 10% of China's arable land has already been contaminated by heavy metal detritus from China's factories, mines, smelters, and power plants.

A second major health issue is the exceedingly high levels of pesticide residues often found in Chinese produce. As documented in the *Journal of Environmental Toxicology and Chemistry,* the underlying problem is the tendency for China's farmers to overuse pesticides in an effort to boost their meager crop yields. As a result, the FDA has had to reject Chinese agricultural products ranging from ginseng and frozen red raspberry crumble to mushrooms.

Beyond the problem of food contamination from banned antibiotics, heavy metals, and pesticides, issues with bacteria and spoilage also arise because of China's lack of an adequate "cold chain." Any country's cold chain begins with refrigerators to cool fruit and vegetables upon harvest. The cold chain extends to refrigerated trucks or rail cars in which the produce can be transported. Still another set of refrigerators and freezers are necessary to store the produce in warehouses before it is shipped to market. On all three counts, China is woefully deficit.

For example, China has only about 30,000 cold storage trucks compared to almost 300,000 in the United States, and its cold storage capacity tops out at a meager 250 million cubic feet. However, according to a study conducted by the consulting firm A.T. Kearney, over the next 10 years, China is going to need about 365,000 refrigerated trucks and 5 *billion* cubic feet of cold storage.

The kinds of contamination problems that arise from the lack of an adequate cold chain are even worse for meat and poultry, as indicated by this passage from the *Wall Street Journal*:

> It's a scene that James Rice, head of the China operations of Tyson Foods Inc., has seen numerous times in his three years with the poultry giant there: tons of featherless, frozen chickens loaded on the backs of flatbed trucks under thick blankets in the summer heat, awaiting a long-haul journey across China. "It's my Achilles heel," says Mr. Rice. He says the lack of everything from temperature-controlled trucks and warehouses to a shortage of general refrigeration know-how limits Tyson to a handful of major cities in China.

Assassins in Toyland

Apparently when you tickle Elmo he's not laughing, he's having a seizure.

—Jay Leno

In an attempt to assure the world's children that millions of Chinese-made toys currently being recalled for containing toxic lead paint and tiny choking hazards can no longer hurt them, high-level Chinese officials announced Tuesday that millions of playthings are being rounded up and immediately put to death.... According to the Xinhua News Agency, *in the past three days alone, factory owners roused an estimated 365,000 Barbie dolls from their dream homes in a violent series of raids. During these raids, the Barbies were separated from their Kens, stripped naked, and had their heads shaved. They were then taken to an undisclosed area, leaned against the wall and shot by a firing squad as toy soldiers were forced to watch.*

—*The Onion*

These satirical treatments of China's toy recall crisis from America's top banana, Jay Leno, and parody newspaper, *The Onion,* provide at least some comic relief from a situation that has been extremely troubling, particularly to parents with young children. Although most people are already well aware of many of the details of this crisis, it is worth at least briefly recapping the extent to which America's toys have been turned into instruments of death by unscrupulous Chinese manufacturers. Here's just a brief scorecard of the kinds of toys that have been recalled from the shelves by the likes of Toys "R" Us, Target, and Wal-Mart:

- 3.8 million Magnetix magnetic building sets that can kill by perforating the intestines if the magnets are swallowed
- 1.5 million Fisher-Price lead-contaminated toys, including popular Sesame Street characters such as Giggle Grabber Soccer Elmo, Chef Dora, Rev & Go Cookie Monster, Ernie and Bert, and Oscar the Grouch
- 1.5 million Thomas & Friends lead-painted wooden trains, and 1 million Hasbro "Easy-Bake" ovens that can trap children's fingers in the oven and burn them
- 253,000 of Mattel's die-cast cars modeled after "Sarge" in the cartoon movie *Cars,* and 90,000 units of Mattel's GeoTrax locomotive line
- 31,000 "Skippy" plastic fish that can break and slash a child's hands, and 15,000 Laugh and Learn Kitchen Toys posing a choking hazard

For concerned parents and grandparents shopping for toys, it is critical to point out that whereas well-known brand companies such as Mattel and Toys "R" Us have had their fair share of bad headlines, the bigger problem is often with those ultra-cheap, "no brand" toys that wind up at deep-discount stores. It is precisely in stores such as these that a variety of Halloween toys have been found to represent far more tricks than treats. Here's just a small sampling:

- 142,000 purple witch buckets, 63,000 green Frankenstein cups, and 55,000 candy-filled skull pails posing a lead hazard
- 120,000 "Creepy Cape" costumes capable of bursting into flames, and 97,000 Mr. Potato Head "Make a Monster Pumpkin" sets deemed a choking hazard

It is precisely these kinds of statistics that raise this overarching question: How can China's toymakers turn something as innocent and pure as children's toys into a profanity of poisons and choking hazards? It is a very good question to which we will return shortly.

Crash Dummies on the Volga

Add another product to the list of Chinese exports whose safety is being called into question: cars. In one of the few crash tests to date of a Chinese-made vehicle outside China, a Chery Amulet sedan's front end folded like a concertina in a recent trial in Moscow. The Russian car magazine that organized the test said it was one of the worst performances ever and called upon Chery Automobile Co. to withdraw the car from the market.

—Wall Street Journal

It's not just agricultural products and low-priced toys and trinkets that consumers have to fear when it comes to the "Made in China" label. As Chinese manufacturers move up the value chain into big-ticket items like automobiles and aircraft and top-line pharmaceuticals, a wide range of consumer risks is emerging.

Consider China's rapidly growing auto industry. It might surprise you to know that China *already* produces more cars than Detroit once you subtract light trucks and SUVs from the equation. However, unlike U.S.-made cars and the cars coming out of Europe and Japan, the safety of many of the Chinese-branded vehicles is exceedingly low.

For example, as indicated in the preceding excerpt, China's Chery Amulet totally flunked its Russian crash test. Another typical data point is offered by the performance—or lack thereof—of the Chinese Brilliance BS6 sedan. In a standard European crash test, the BS6 sedan was driven at 40 miles per hour straight into a barrier. As described by analyst Chris Haak, the results were right out of a Ralph Nader nightmare:

> In cars that ace these tests, the passenger compartment stays almost completely intact with no intrusion of the floor into the driver's foot well or the instrument panel into the driver's face. The best cars often still have functioning driver's doors, yet sacrifice so much of their front end absorbing the crash energy that the occupants get out of the car relatively unscathed.

> Instead, the poorly named Brilliance BS6 saw the pedals intrude into the driver's space by 18 inches, and the dashboard by 7 inches. The driver's door wouldn't open without the technicians using a huge crowbar, and the rocker panel bent almost 90°, and stopped only when it hit the floor. The base of the windshield moved to the same vertical plane as the top of the windshield was before the crash, and the driver was left sharing space with the steering wheel, windshield, and the front end of the car. He or she would have almost certainly been killed instantly.

Perhaps the worst aspect of China's "unsafe at any speed" auto industry is China's use of both Latin America and Africa as dumping grounds for cheap cars that would pass neither emissions or safety tests in European or U.S. markets. While these cheap cars are very attractive to lower income buyers, they are nothing but rolling death-traps and pollution factories. Nor are the Chinese particularly coy about this. As Zheng Guoqing, the head of sales to Africa for the Great Wall Motor Co. has soft-pedaled it: "The performance-price ratio of our products is high so African people like our brand. The emissions standard is not particularly high there. The requirement for safety is also not high."

The Origins of China's Flood of Contaminated, Defective, and Cancerous Products

Many of the "Southern-style" catfish fillets on U.S. grocery shelves these days are indeed from the South—of China. The Chinese government's own reports express alarm that many rivers in this region are so contaminated with heavy metals from industrial byproducts and pesticides including DDT, that they are too dangerous to touch, much less raise fish in.

—Washington Post

At this point, it is critical to ask: Just why are Chinese products so unsafe over such a wide range of product categories? In their defense, Chinese officials routinely argue that their products are as safe as any other country in the world. Cold, hard statistics tell a very different story. China's failure rate consistently outpaces its market share over a wide range of products across a number of countries and continents.

In Japan, for example, China accounts for about a third of all contaminated foods but accounts for only 15% of Japan's food imports. Similarly in Europe, almost half of all defective products identified by European Union regulators come from China. A fourth of these defective products are Chinese-made toys, but other products range from electrical appliances and cars to lighting equipment and cosmetics. This pattern holds equally true in the United States. China accounts for 60% of all consumer-product recalls in the United States and nearly all of its toy recalls—far outpacing the failure rates of other developing countries such as Brazil and Mexico on a market-share adjusted basis.

The Bait-and-Switch Quality Fade

Some quality issues are not all that serious, but others are downright frightening. One of the most disturbing examples I have encountered while working in China involved the manufacture and importation of aluminum systems used to construct high-rise commercial buildings. These are the systems that support tons of concrete as it is being poured, and their general stability is critical.

The American company that designed and patented the system engineered all key components. It knew exactly how much each part was supposed to weigh, and yet the level of engineering sophistication did not stop the supplier from making a unilateral decision to reduce the specifications. When the "production error" was caught, one aluminum part was found to be weighing less than 90% of its intended weight. Where did the missing aluminum go? Into the factory owner's pocket as a cost saving. The only thing passed on to the customer was an increase in product risk.

—Forbes.com

One of the most important reasons for the high failure rates of Chinese products is a variation on the old tactic of "bait and switch" known as the *quality fade.* Here's how it works:

An American, European, or Japanese company goes to China to offshore the production of its product. A Chinese company wins the order by producing a prototype of the desired product *exactly* to the specifications of the offshoring company. That's the "bait."

The switch comes sometime after the Chinese company begins mass producing the product. At some point, after it has gained the confidence of its foreign client, the Chinese company begins cutting costs by substituting inferior materials and/or altering the design. If the foreign company does not have adequate safeguards in place to detect the quality fade, the result of this quality switch can be disastrous.

A telling case in point is the "Aqua Dots–date rape drug" fiasco described earlier. The toy's distributor, Australia's Moose Enterprises, lost millions of dollars in sales and took a very heavy hit to its brand name in the wake of this scandal. The company's investigation eventually led it to a Chinese factory that it had contracted for production. In classic and deadly quality fade, the factory managers substituted the toxic date rape chemical for a safe glue during manufacturing—all to make a few extra bucks.

Silence of the Whistleblowing Lambs

If you want to have a good system of consumer protection, protecting whistleblowers is an essential requirement.

—Wang Hai, Chinese consumer rights advocate

There are no gold stars awarded in China for whistleblowing—a critical policing mechanism in any supply chain for consumer protection. Instead, the much more likely result for employees who publicly expose flaws in their companies' products is jail, a terrible beating, or both. The grim fates of three whistleblowers in China, as documented by the *Financial Times*, graphically illustrates the extreme dangers:

The first whistleblower, Dr. Tang Zhixiong, accused his fellow doctors of conducting unethical transplant surgeries. In addition, Ms. Zhou Huanxi and Mr. Shi Yuefu each separately denounced their former companies for producing fake medicines.

Dr. Tang is now on the run after receiving violent threats, and he fears arrest on trumped up charges. Dr. Tang's fear of arrest is hardly unfounded. After Ms. Zhou revealed that a tonic being marketed to pregnant women as a health enhancer was nothing but snake oil, she was arrested on a phony charge of blackmail and jailed for almost four years. Meanwhile, Mr. Shi was not quite as "lucky" as Dr. Tang and Ms. Zhou. He was run over by a van with a bogus license plate and left with serious brain injuries.

First We Kill All the Trial Lawyers

Although "ambulance-chasing" trial lawyers are often ridiculed and reviled in America, the fear of multimillion-dollar lawsuits undeniably leads to more socially responsible corporate behavior. In contrast, it is almost impossible for Chinese citizens or injured consumers outside of China to sue Chinese companies making contaminated or defective products. As noted in *Fortune* magazine, "While suing companies in foreign countries is always more difficult than pursuing a domestic lawsuit, the complexities of filing a case against a Chinese firm are compounded by the country's regulatory and legal systems and by political relations between Washington and Beijing. As one lawyer put it, 'You're spitting into the wind.'"

Indeed, when sued, Chinese companies often simply do not show up to U.S. courts; and it's next to impossible to get access to any of their records. Pinning these companies down is further complicated by the fact that their headquarters are often simply bare-bones operations—glorified fronts for purveying their poison. Nor do any mutual agreements between the United States and China enforce legal judgments. By some estimates, a lawsuit against a Chinese company takes at least ten years and costs five times as much to prosecute. Only big companies can afford to pay that much and wait that long. Everybody else is out of luck.

That Cold Black Heart—A Poison-for-Profit Culture

Actions from the top down will not solve this problem, because the problem goes much deeper than Beijing. There still remains that uneasy question lurking in the shadows of

China's rapid growth: Why would so many people be willing to cut corners to make an extra dollar, even at the cost of human lives?

—Emily Parker

Perhaps the most unsettling and controversial part of the "Made Badly in China" problem is framed in the words of Emily Parker in the preceding excerpt. This is the possibility that in the godless state of China, far too many entrepreneurs lack the ethical fiber and moral compass to do anything other than to try to make a buck any way they can—no matter what the health and safety consequences for their consumers. In this regard, the World Christian Database reports that China has by far the largest percentage of "unbelievers" in the world.

Two high-profile cases illustrate how the cold, black, godless hearts of at least some Chinese entrepreneurs strongly suggest the absence of any moral compass in China's "poison-for-profit" culture.

One such case involves the recall of almost half a million "killer tires" made by the Hangzhou Zhongce Rubber Company. At some point in the production process, in a classic quality fade, this Chinese manufacturer began leaving out an important safety feature called the "gum strip" to further boost its profit margin. This 0.6mm layer of rubber is added to steel-belt radial tires to prevent tread separation. The inevitable result of leaving out the gum strips is exploding tires that can kill a family of four in an SUV faster than a drunk driver on a Saturday night.

A second case that similarly illustrates China's poison-for-profit culture involves the oft-reported case of the spiking of pet food with the chemical melamine. This heinous act killed as many as 40,000 pets in America; and it's critical to explain just exactly why the Chinese manufacturers added melamine to the pet food mix.

Melamine is an acutely toxic organic chemical that has little or no nutritional value. It was added to the pet food for one simple reason:

to *falsely* give the appearance of higher protein levels in the feed so that the feed could command a higher price. American pets and their owners paid a very high price indeed.

Of Corporations and Consumers with Eyes Wide Shut

While China's government officials and entrepreneurs must shoulder much of the blame for the "Made Badly in China" problem, at least some of that blame must fall on consumers as well as on those American, European, and other foreign companies that outsource their production to China.

On the corporate front, the sad fact is that foreign companies that outsource to China often do not install adequate quality-control systems. That's exactly why a company such as Mattel got quickly neck deep in a toy recall involving tens of millions of toys. As Professor Shih-fen Chen described that particular event, "We are not talking about a few random errors in production that escaped the eyes of quality-control managers, but about a colossal failure of the outsourcing firm that let 19 million pieces of unsafe toys slip into the marketplace."

As for consumers, most buyers focus on *product brand* rather than *country of origin* when making their product choices. In other words, we buy Chinese iPods, Chinese Barbie dolls, and Chinese spark plugs not because we trust China but because we trust Apple, Mattel, and Bosch. That's a buying strategy all of us need to seriously rethink!

4

The "Blood and Nukes for Oil" Wars— The Sum of All Chinese Fears

Throughout the summer and into the fall of 1941, Japanese negotiators and the United States were at loggerheads. The U.S.-led oil embargo would not be suspended until the Japanese stopped their militaristic expansion. ... By September 1941, Japanese reserves had dropped to 50 million barrels, and their navy alone was burning 2,900 barrels of oil every hour. The Japanese had reached a crossroads. If they did nothing, they would be out of oil and options in less than two years. If they chose war, there was a good chance they could lose a protracted conflict. Given the possibility of success with the second option versus none with the first option, the Japanese chose war.

—Lieutenant Colonel Patrick H. Donovan, U.S. Air Force

It might come as a surprise to many Americans that it was America in 1941 and not the Arabs in 1973 that imposed the world's first oil embargo. Uncle Sam abruptly cut off Japan's imported oil in response to Japan's brutal invasion of China.

America's attempt to pressure Japan to withdraw from China constituted a deep humiliation to a country with a premium on "saving face." It also left the Japanese military with a petroleum reserve that would be quickly exhausted—and some say, little choice but to attack Pearl Harbor and wage war on the United States.

Today, oil remains the lifeblood of every modern economy, and considerable blood continues to be shed in the Middle East, Africa, and elsewhere to control or protect the vast network that brings this "black gold" from faraway places to the world's factories and transportation systems. What is disturbingly new about today's "blood for oil" wars is China's emerging and highly disruptive role.

China's rapidly expanding thirst for petroleum has not only sent gas prices and the price of a barrel of oil soaring. China's brass-knuckled, amoral approach to securing its oil reserves is facilitating such tragedies as the slaughter of Burmese protestors and the Darfur genocide. China's willingness to trade "blood and nukes for oil" is also rapidly accelerating the global arms race and nuclear proliferation.

An (Oil Price) Shocking Global Recession?

At the end of the day, you've got two very large consumers [the United States and China] competing over the same sandbox.

—Gal Luft, Institute for the Analysis of Global Security

Any discussion of China's growing thirst for oil must first acknowledge that the biggest guzzler of global oil is the United States. With less than 5% of the world's population, the United States annually consumes about 25% of the world's oil production. In comparison, with fully 20% of the world's population, China currently consumes only about 7% of the world's oil. However, as China's economy continues to grow rapidly, so, too, will its oil consumption and share of the world oil market—even as the U.S. share of that market falls. The most salient facts are these:

- China is the world's second-largest petroleum consumer behind only the United States, and its oil demand is projected to *triple* by 2030.

- China is already heavily dependent on oil imports, importing more than 40% of its needs, and its oil import dependence is projected to reach 60% by 2020.

Because of surging oil demand in China and other emerging economies, such as India, the International Monetary Fund is now warning of a highly inflationary "permanent oil price shock" and a possible sustained global recession over the next several decades induced by this price shock. While the developed nations of the world such as the United States, Germany, and Japan will be hurt by these oil price shocks, it will be the poverty-stricken developing countries—from Bangladesh and Cambodia to Haiti and Mexico—that will be hurt even more.

Despite the serious economic impacts of inflation and recession that may result from China's increasing participation in world oil markets, it is China's highly provocative energy security strategies and their far-ranging geopolitical effects that may ultimately prove to be most dangerous to global economic and political stability. To understand these effects, it is first useful to understand China's deepest oil-security fear: the threat of a U.S. oil embargo or other type of oil-supply disruption.

The Sum of All Chinese Oil Fears

Energy is vital to a country's security and material well-being. A state unable to provide its people with adequate energy supplies often resorts to force.

—Senator Richard Lugar and Former CIA Director James Woolsey

The oil China currently imports from the Middle East and Africa is still transported through ... the Strait of Malacca. This single route will bring certain strategic risks. Once China and Southeast Asian countries or the United States fall foul of each other, oil transportation will be impeded.

—*China's People's Daily*

Today's China is the largest economy without a substantial strategic petroleum reserve and *the* most vulnerable to oil-market disruptions. In fact, China has on hand less than ten days of supply versus about 60 days for the United States and 100 days for Japan.

Given this vulnerability, the paramount energy security fear of China is that the United States might attempt to do what it once did to Japan—embargo China's oil supplies as a means of exerting pressure on Chinese economic, trade, or foreign policies. This is not an unreasonable fear, at least from the Chinese perspective.

The most likely, but hardly the only, U.S. oil-embargo scenario would involve a Chinese invasion of Taiwan. As discussed in more detail in Chapter 10, "Red Army Rising—The Coming China Hot Wars," China has made it clear to the world community that this "renegade province" belongs to the Chinese mainland. Should Taiwan continue to resist China or, far more provocatively, officially declare its independence, a blitzkrieg-style invasion of the island is certainly well within the scope of Chinese military plans.

Of course, one of the most logical strategic responses of the United States to such an invasion would be to block the very narrow Strait of Malacca. This key chokepoint links the Indian and Pacific Oceans and provides passage for about 80% of China's oil imports. Blocking this narrow strait would effectively cut off China's oil-supply lifeline.

China's Provocative "Zero Sum" Oil-Supply Game

With its overriding goal of securing oil and gas to fuel China's economic growth, the Chinese government has actively cultivated its relations with the oil-rich Middle East, especially Iran and Saudi Arabia. In their dogged pursuit of this goal, Chinese policymakers have been more than willing not only to undercut U.S. [nuclear] nonproliferation efforts but also to work closely with governments that export Islamic [terrorism].

—Dan Blumenthal, *Middle East Quarterly*

How has China sought to strategically address its oil-security fears? At the heart of its hard-edged strategy is a "zero sum" approach that is radically different from that of the United States. Whereas the United States focuses on ensuring the security of the international oil market, China has adopted a "bilateral contracting approach" in which it seeks to lock down the physical supplies of oil-producing countries. By locking down these physical supplies for themselves, China essentially locks out other nations. In essence, this brass-knuckled strategy is designed to obtain *physical* control rather than merely financial control of the oil *before* it ever gets to market.

Locking other nations out of the world's oil supplies is hardly the worst feature of China's oil-security strategy. That distinction is reserved for China's own self-professed amoral approach to securing the oil reserves it pursues. Symptomatic of this approach, everyone from China's business leaders right up to its president and premier openly boasts to dictators and rogue states alike that China will never condition its oil and other natural resource deals on any moral principle or human rights issues that challenge the sovereignty of its trading partners. China's President Hu Jintao has succinctly summarized China's amoral doctrine: "Just business, no political conditions."

Under this amoral doctrine, China has been quite willing to engage in what the U.S.-China Commission has dryly described as "nonmarket reciprocity" by cutting deals with some of the most dangerous rogue nations in the world. In some deals, China trades weapons of mass destruction, including highly sophisticated ballistic missiles, in return for oil. In other deals, China trades sensitive nuclear weapons technology for oil.

Arguably the worst feature of China's amoral brand of foreign policy is its commercial use of its U.N. veto as a bargaining chip to secure access to the oil resources of numerous rogue and terrorist nations. China has this veto power because it is a permanent member of the U.N. Security Council. Each permanent member has such veto power, and it only takes the veto of one member to block any type of U.N. sanctions or the use of U.N. peacekeeping troops.

Given the broader humanitarian goals of the United Nations and its peacekeeping mission, China's crass commercial use of its U.N. veto power is nothing short of despicable. That it has resulted in the human misery of millions should be evident in the following examples involving genocide in Darfur, the brutal suppression of pro-democracy forces in Burma, the transfer of weapons-grade nuclear technologies to Iran, and the looting of Angola.

The Vetoing Panda Proliferates Genocide in Darfur

All summer, the U.N. Security Council debated whether to condemn the Sudanese government for supporting the murderous Janjaweed militias in Darfur.... Quietly but steadfastly, China's ambassador to the United Nations, Wang Guangya, has helped defang U.S.-sponsored drafts against Sudan, transforming language threatening to "take further action" against Khartoum into the more benign "consider taking additional measures."... Beijing's goal? Probably to

protect its investments in the Sudanese oil industry, including
a 40% stake in a refinery pumping more than 300,000 barrels
a day and a 1500-kilometer pipeline from Sudan to the
Red Sea.

—*The New Republic*

Since 2003, the black African farmers of Darfur in the Sudan
have been subject to one of the most brutal campaigns of rape, sys-
tematic starving, and genocide ever witnessed. This campaign of
ethnic cleansing has been waged by fierce nomadic Arab tribes and
their Janjaweed militia forces against the black Africans. The Arab
Janjaweed militia has, in turn, been armed and supported militarily
by the Arab-based Sudanese government.

At the root of the Darfur conflict is a severe drought and desertification brought on by global warming. These conditions have pushed
the nomadic Arab tribes deep into Darfur in search of land and water,
and these Arab tribes and their militia forces have taken both from
the black Africans in a brutal display of might over right. To date,
hundreds of thousands of black Africans have been killed and more
than two million have been driven off their land into refugee camps.

Much of the blood shed to date in Darfur is on the hands of the
Chinese government. For the first four years of conflict, China steadfastly refused to allow the United Nations either to impose sanctions
against the Sudan or to land a substantial peacekeeping force. In
exchange for China's diplomatic shield, the Sudan has responded by
making China its biggest oil customer.

To pay for that oil, China has also emerged as the Sudan's largest
supplier of weapons. Indeed, it has been Chinese-made tanks, fighter
planes, bombers, machine guns, helicopters, and rocket-propelled
grenades that have often been used in the campaign of genocide
in Darfur.

Under the threat of a possible boycott of the 2008 Beijing Olympics, China finally agreed to support the insertion of a U.N. peacekeeping force. Much of the damage in Darfur has, however, already been done as the Arab tribes have almost completely displaced the black Africans in many areas of Darfur.

The Oil-Thirsty Panda Sacrifices Burmese Monks on the Altar of Energy Security

Burma's military junta has been showing its true colors this week, firing automatic weapons at peaceful demonstrators and raiding monasteries to beat and kill Buddhist monks. But the junta's criminal disdain for human rights has also cast a harsh light on China, the principal commercial partner, strategic ally, and diplomatic protector of the junta. While protesters were being shot in Burma, China was preventing the United Nations Security Council from considering sanctions on the killers—or even issuing a condemnation of the junta's use of lethal force.

—*Boston Globe*

In September 2007, the long-suffering Burmese people rose up in protest over rising energy prices. These protests quickly morphed into a broader plea for a return to a democratic system, which had been smashed in 1990 by a military coup d'état.

Burma's military junta ruthlessly responded to these peaceful protests by slaughtering thousands of Burmese citizens, killing a foreign journalist, and quite literally caging the Buddhist monks and nuns who helped lead the protests behind barbwire enclosures.

Just like in Darfur, this Burmese blood is on the hands of the Chinese government. When the United Nations attempted action on the Burmese question, China used its veto power to prevent any meaningful U.N. intervention.

As to why China would want to protect Burma's dictators, it is yet another "blood for oil" deal. China not only wants to import the lion's share of Burma's natural gas reserves, which measure over half a trillion cubic meters. Far more important strategically is China's plan to build a $2 billion oil pipeline from Burma's coast on the Bay of Bengal to China's Yunnan Province.

The Burma-China pipeline is a critical project because it would allow China to take delivery of oil from the Middle East without passing through the very narrow Strait of Malacca. As noted earlier, this is a key chokepoint that could easily be shut down by the U.S. Navy in time of conflict.

The WMD Panda Trades Weapons and Nukes for Oil

Beijing has sold thousands of tanks, artillery pieces, and armored personnel carriers to Iran, more than 100 combat aircraft, and dozens of small warships. Beijing has also sold Iran an array of missile systems and technology, including air-to-air missiles, surface-to-air missiles, and antishipping cruise missiles. Most worrisome have been China's transfer of ballistic missile technology and its assistance with Iran's [nuclear] programs. ... China has sent entire factories to Iran for producing chemicals that, although they have legitimate purposes, can also be used to make poison gas, and tons of industrial chemicals that could be used in making nerve agents.

—The Rand Corporation

As a "charter member" of President George W. Bush's "axis of evil," Iran possesses the world's second-largest natural gas reserves after Russia and controls fully 10% of the world's oil reserves. Perhaps not surprisingly, oil export revenues account for 80% to 90% of the country's total export earnings.

Today, Iran's flood of oil revenues is funding roughly half of Iran's government budget, and much of this budget is devoted to the purchase of advanced weapons systems from China. Chinese weaponry ranges from Silkworm missiles capable of striking ships in the Strait of Hormuz and surface to air missiles able to knock commercial or military planes out of the sky to a wide variety of conventional arms and even armor-piercing bullets.

The China-Iran weapons bazaar is hardly open simply for Iran's self-defense. According to the U.S. State Department, Iran's radical fundamentalist Shiite Muslim regime has consistently been the most active state sponsor of terrorism. It is also a key destabilizing force in Iraq.

Iran's successful efforts to destabilize Iraq begin with its considerable influence over the majority Shiite population in Iraq and their radical Mullah militias. Iran also acts as a haven for Al Qaeda terrorists and is a launching point for insurgent activity into Iraq. In addition, covert Iranian operatives continue to smuggle Chinese-made weapons into Iraq. As previously noted, this arsenal includes armor-piercing bullets that can slice through the Kevlar vests of American soldiers faster than a knife through butter.

Most dangerously for the region and world, China is also playing a key role in Iran's quest to develop its nuclear capabilities. Historically, it has been China that has provided both the expertise and technology. Even now, as Chinese government officials continue to deny ongoing nuclear assistance, Chinese companies, with tacit government support, regularly smuggle sensitive materials and equipment into Iran's nuclear sector.

Should Iran eventually join the nuclear club, one potential trigger for a Middle East Armageddon is Iran's promise to nuke Israel out of existence. That Israel likely has its own arsenal of nuclear weapons with which to swiftly retaliate seems to have been lost on the Iranians.

A second potential trigger for war is the growing tension in the region between the Shiite Muslim states led by Iran and the predominantly Sunni Muslim states that include Saudi Arabia, Jordan, the United Arab Emirates, and Egypt. If Iran were to succeed in developing nuclear weapons, this could spark a nuclear arms race whereby both the Saudis and Egyptians would feel compelled to join the nuclear club.

Faced with these growing dangers, the United States, Germany, France, Great Britain, and Japan have tried to counter Iran's rogue behavior by seeking to impose tough economic sanctions. However, attempts to impose these sanctions have been largely unsuccessful for one very simple reason: China. The following passage from the *Middle East Quarterly* by Dan Blumenthal graphically illustrates why China is the problem and how China uses its U.N. veto to secure access to huge oil and natural gas reserves like Iran's massive Yadavaran field. This field contains up to three billion barrels of recoverable reserves and a total production capacity of as much as 300,000 barrels a day:

> Chinese foreign minister Li Zhaoxing flew to Tehran to conclude an oil and gas deal [for Yadavaran] between China's state-owned Sinopec and the Iranian oil ministry worth approximately $100 billion over thirty years. The purpose of Li's visit was clearly to exploit tensions between Washington and Tehran over Iran's nuclear program. His trip came against the backdrop of delicate European Union-led negotiations with Iran over its nuclear program and U.S. threats to refer the Iranian nuclear matter to the United Nations Security Council. After the oil deal was signed, Li announced that *China would refuse to refer the issue of Iran's nuclear program to the Security Council.*

China's sanction-killing support for Iran has had two extremely unfortunate effects. First, it has helped prop up a regime that is so highly unpopular among much of the populace *that it might have otherwise collapsed by now*. Second, China's willingness to undercut economic sanctions against Iran has resulted in Japan and many European nations essentially "throwing in the sanctions towel" and seeking to make their own business deals with Iran. Their clear argument: We cannot stand by as China locks down all the best undeveloped petroleum reserves.

The Dissembling Panda Facilitates Corruption and Looting in Angola

> *Angola presents a horrifying case of squandered possibilities. Rich in oil and diamonds, this country on the southwestern coast of Africa is desperately poor. In the first few years of this decade, corruption was so extreme that each year, more than $1 billion of Angola's oil revenues reportedly disappeared.*

—Professor John McMillan

Angola suffers from a severe case of what economists call the "natural resource curse": The greater a country's natural resources, the more likely it is that the country's corrupt rulers will try to capture this wealth for their own Swiss bank accounts rather than use those natural resources riches on behalf of the people. Nowhere is this more true than in Angola.

In a concerted diplomatic effort to free Angola of its natural resource curse, the United States, the International Monetary Fund, and the World Bank have all called for greater transparency in the tracking of Angola's oil revenues. However, the biggest obstacle to reform has been China and its willingness to deal secretly with Angola's corrupt leadership.

In exchange for oil-drilling rights in Angola, China regularly shells out huge upfront payments to Angolan officials that are impossible to track. China also provides lavish "soft loans" to the Angolan government, much of which quickly bypass the public treasury for off-shore accounts or are funneled into the campaign coffers of the ruling party to help keep it in power. As a result of these Angolan-Chinese connections, Angola is now China's top energy supplier. As reported by Global Witness, China's shame in this matter is that, despite Angola's vast natural resource wealth, one in four of Angolan children die before the age of five and almost 10% of the Angolan people remain dependent on international food aid.

A Coming "Hot War" on the Asian High Seas?

It should be clear from each of the previous examples just how far China will go to ensure its energy security. To end this chapter, it is useful to reflect on how China's growing oil appetite might also put it into conflict with several of its key Asian neighbors. One such conflict is taking place in the South China Sea over oil reserves beneath the contested Spratly and Paracel island chains.

The Disputed Spratly and Paracel Island Chains

Just when it seemed China and Vietnam had buried their con-flicting claims to the Spratly Islands, Beijing is contesting a new Hanoi-tendered, BP-led, U.S. $2 billion natural-gas proj-ect near the rocky group of islands and reefs in the South China Sea. The flare-up marks perhaps the strongest indica-tion yet that Beijing's soft-power overtures toward Southeast Asia are hardening when it comes to energy-security con-cerns. ... Relations between neighboring Vietnam and China have long been tense, including recent armed skirmishes in the late 1970s and '80s. The two sides fought a brief but bloody border war in the wake of Vietnam's invasion of Cambodia, which ousted the Beijing-backed Khmer Rouge

*regime. In 1988, Vietnam and China fought a brief naval bat-
tle over the contested Spratly Islands in the south-central
area of the South China Sea.*

—*Asia Times Online*

The Paracel and Spratly island chains are little more than rocks
and reefs in the South China Sea, but together they sit atop potentially significant oil reserves. The Paracels are roughly equidistant
from China, Vietnam, and the Philippines. Both China and Vietnam
as well as Taiwan lay claim to the islands. However, it is China that
actually commands the Paracel turf. In 1974, China took advantage of
the ongoing civil war between South and North Vietnam to overrun a
garrison on the Paracels manned by South Vietnamese troops, and
China has held this position to this day—over the strenuous protests
of the Vietnamese government.

The Spratly Islands are laid claim to by China and Vietnam as
well as Malaysia, the Philippines, and Taiwan, and similarly consist of
a large number of small islands and reefs. These islands are likewise
thought to contain significant oil and gas reserves, perhaps as large of
reserves as the Arab kingdom of Kuwait. This would place the
Spratlys as the fourth largest reserve bed in the world—a prize well
worth fighting for.

As in the Paracels Islands, China has engaged in military clashes
with Vietnam over the Spratlys while China, Malaysia, the Philippines, Taiwan, and Vietnam all have military forces scattered
throughout the area. Should substantial oil and gas reserves actually
be discovered in the region, an escalation of the currently relatively
low-intensity conflict would be inevitable.

❖　❖　❖　❖　❖

In this chapter, we have seen how China's rapidly growing thirst
for oil is creating a host of conflicts and problems around the globe—
from the brutal slaughter of monks in Burma and a campaign of

genocide in Darfur to increasing instability in the Middle East and the looting of Africa. One common reprehensible thread in this whole sordid story is China's crass commercial use of its U.N. veto to quite literally trade blood and nukes for oil.

In the next chapter, we examine an equally reprehensible practice by China to secure other natural resources to feed and fuel its heavy manufacturing model—from alumina, copper, and iron ore to paper, rubber, and teak. This practice involves a twenty-first century brand of imperialism that would make Lenin and Mao turn over in their graves.

5

The World's Most Ironic Imperialist and Weapons of Mass Construction

People say China is a sleeping giant, but it's wide awake. It's the elephant creeping up behind us. Only, it's so big we can scarcely see it moving.

—Zainab Bangura, Sierra Leone political activist

In 1916, Vladimir Lenin, a forefather of Chinese communism, described *imperialism* as the "highest form of capitalism." The goal of the imperialist nation is to use its superior financial resources and managerial expertise to gain economic control over the minerals, raw materials, agricultural products, and other natural resources of the imperialized country. Such control is typically achieved by lavishly bribing the corrupt rulers of the developing nation who facilitate the influx of capital, skilled labor, and managerial talent from the imperialist country.

This first wave of capital and labor constitutes the imperialist's "weapons of mass construction." These weapons are used to build the transportation and communications networks and the extraction infrastructures that will be needed for the subsequent "natural resource rape."

Once the imperialist nation gains control of the resources, it ships them back to the home country to feed its industrial machine. While the exploited country is stripped of its wealth and sees its environment degraded, the imperialist country produces high valued-added, finished goods that it exports to world markets. It thereby earns, in Lenin's terms, "super profits," on the backs of the poor in the imperialized country.

In the Marxist-Leninist view, this is arguably what the imperialistic British Empire did in its colonial heyday in its relations with East African colonies such as Kenya and Uganda. France also did it in West African colonies such as the Ivory Coast, Guinea, Mali, and Senegal. Before African independence, even lesser nations such as Belgium and Portugal got into the imperialist act in places such as the Congo, Angola, and Mozambique.

Today, however, in a supreme historical irony, there is a new imperialist on the African block preying on many of those former colonies. It is none other than one of the loudest critics and worst former victims of British and Japanese imperialism: the putatively Marxist-Leninist People's Republic of China. Throughout Africa, Latin America, and Asia, China is using the Trojan horse of a "South-South" message that allies China in a workers' coalition with other developing countries against "northern hemisphere" imperialists such as the United States, France, Russia, and Great Britain. Under the cover of this South-South diplomacy, China is deploying a potent mix of state-subsidized capital, managerial expertise, and skilled labor, and is rapidly gaining economic control of a lion's share of the world's metals, minerals, raw materials, and agricultural resources.

The unwitting developing countries now ensnared in China's South-South imperialistic web are starting to have an increasingly rude and painful awakening. At the root of China's new imperialism is a voracious economic appetite for resources and raw materials.

The Heavy Appetites of China's Heavy Manufacturing Model

Chinese geologists estimate that the demand for minerals over the next 30 years may exceed product by as much as a factor of five. The projections are staggering: 5.3–6.8 million tons of copper by 2023 and 13 million tons of aluminum by 2028.

—Asia Pacific Bulletin

In choosing to be the "factory floor" of the world, China has hitched its star to a heavy manufacturing model that, in less than three short decades, has transformed the country from a quiet agricultural backwater into one of the world's largest consumers of metals, minerals, lumber, and other raw materials. China's strategy is different from that other emerging behemoth, India, which is focusing much less on heavy manufacturing and much more on software, global service industries, and other information technology niches.

Pursuing its heavy manufacturing model, China now uses half of the world's cement, one-third of its steel, one-fourth of its copper, and one-fifth of its aluminum. China is also one of the top consumers of Thai rubber, Burmese teak, Chilean and Philippine copper, cobalt from the Congo, and Indonesian pulp and paper. Other minerals high on China's list but low in the consciousness of the general public range from "industrial minerals" such as limestone, dolomite, phosphate rock, and sulfur to "process minerals" such as titanium slag and phosphoric acid.

China's strategy for securing these production inputs is similar to that for oil. China seeks to gain as tight a *physical* control of these resources as possible. The way China gains ownership control is by first ingratiating itself to foreign governments and then encircling the country's economy with nearly every strategy described by Lenin in the "imperialist playbook."

In the first stage of China's relationship with a developing country, China dangles lavish, low-interest loans as bait and uses its huge army of engineers and laborers to help the country build up its infrastructure—from roads and dams to hotels and stadiums, from parliament buildings and palaces to satellite capabilities and telecommunications networks. In this regard, over the past few decades, more than a thousand Chinese firms, private and state owned, have been deployed to the overseas construction market along with an estimated three million construction workers. Backed by heavily subsidized, low-interest loans from the government—the financial capital described by Lenin—both state-owned and private Chinese construction firms are able to penetrate these overseas markets. As noted in the *Far Eastern Economic Review,* the Chinese government then "uses the funding to gain political and economic leverage in developing countries, as well as to encourage the purchase of Chinese equipment and labor."

In some cases, such as the Sudan and Burma, China also sells weaponry to the country as a means of ensuring continued political control by the ruling elites it courts. In the worst cases, China offers political favors ranging from the use of its veto at the United Nations to threatening retaliation if the United States, Europe, or Japan engages in any type of economic embargoes aimed at curbing human rights abuses or violations of democratic freedoms.

The Chinese diplomatic approach has great appeal to many Africans, who for decades felt the colonial/imperialist yoke of European nations. As Zhou Wenzhong, the assistant deputy foreign minister in China, has succinctly described this seductive message in the case of the Sudanese genocide in Darfur: "I think the internal situation in the Sudan is an internal affair, and we are not in a position to impose upon them. You have tried to impose a market economy and multiparty democracy on these countries, which are not ready for it. We are also against embargoes, which you have tried to use against us."

These various economic and diplomatic gambits by China not only build "goodwill" between the two countries, they also provide ample opportunity for China to enrich the developing country's ruling elites through favors and bribes and thereby directly win their favor. In many cases, China is also able to tie the loans it makes directly to claims on the country's actual raw materials. China also insists on deals that open the country's markets to Chinese exports, often wiping out domestic industries in the process.

Of course, the investments made in highway systems and communications quite literally and digitally pave the way for precisely the kind of "high-low" trade that China is seeking. When completed, the next stage of the relationship kicks in. This is when China directs its financial capital and human resources to the development of the extraction and harvesting activities and transport of the natural resources back home for the production of higher value-added goods. One of the useful by-products of this relationship is to provide considerable employment opportunities for Chinese workers. In this way, China's weapons of mass construction and global economic strategy also act as a political safety valve at home.

In effect, China is using foreign aid and the promise of capital investment to leverage one-sided "joint ventures" for massive resource extraction operations. In the process, it systematically strips nations of their raw materials and natural resources while recovering the costs of these materials and resources by dumping cheap finished goods into these same countries, often driving out local labor and driving up the local unemployment rate. Let's first look at how this scenario is playing out with chilling effectiveness on the African continent.

Heart of Darkness—China's Parasitic African Safari

We should unite and drive U.S. imperialism from Asia, Africa and Latin America back to where it came from.

—Mao Zedong

China and Africa formally started their economic relationship in 1414 in the most spectacular of fashions. With great fanfare, the emperor of the Ming Dynasty dispatched a fleet of more than 60 galleons with crews of more than 30,000 to the "Dark Continent" on a mission of trade and exploration. This initial round of China-African trade also started in the most fair, equal, and promising of ways—with a pair of magical giraffes gifted to Chinese explorers by African leaders and the opening of trade routes that saw African tortoiseshell, elephant ivory, and rhinoceros-horn medicine exchanged for Chinese gold, silk, and spices.

The relationship was short-lived. When the emperor died, China quickly withdrew into an isolationist foreign policy. Five *centuries* passed before the Chinese government would again take an active interest in Africa.

The new China-Africa relationship began during the 1960s shortly after Mao formally broke with the Soviet Union. In seeking to provide a strategic counterweight to both the United States and the Soviet Union, Mao threw the full weight of China's resources behind the various revolutionary and independence movements in Africa.

In many countries, the Chinese helped arm and train rebels. They sent doctors and nurses. They also helped educate thousands of African students in both Chinese universities and local schools using imported Chinese teachers.

Perhaps most important in currying African favor and cultivating goodwill was China's first deployment in Africa of its "weapons of mass construction." Thousands of Chinese contractors and engineers helped build strategic infrastructure, such as the TanZam railway linking Tanzania to Zambia. This railway played a key role in isolating the then-apartheid South Africa.

Chinese contractors also built stadiums for soccer and political rallies and other so-called prestige projects. The goal during this Cold War era was to build solidarity with the new, anti-imperial regimes and spread communism.

Fast-forward 30 years, and these purely ideologically motivated efforts now are bearing a sweet economic fruit for China. In the 1990s, after a significant withdrawal from Africa in the 1980s to tend to its own struggling economy, China began to return to Africa in force. This time, however, China's business in Africa was to be just that, purely business. Its strategic goal was nothing less than gaining full economic control of the metals, minerals, raw materials, and agricultural riches of a continent that is as wealthy in these resources as it is lacking in political and social structures to defend itself from the imperialistic Chinese assault.

As another economic gift from China's earlier ideological days in Africa, many of the same rebels who China had supported were now waiting with trusting, and unsuspecting, open arms for this new wave of Chinese emissaries and entrepreneurs. A select but important few had even wound up in high positions in governments across the continent. Many of these now-middle-aged rebels had also exchanged their military uniforms and camouflage for three-piece business suits. Former rebels were standing side by side with thousands of former students who had joined the elite economic classes using the currency of their Chinese-subsidized education.

Today, as U.S. former Assistant Secretary of State for African Affairs Walter Kansteiner has put it, "China has simply exploded into Africa," and China now has a significant presence in all 54 African nations.

Benevolent Bootstrap or Imperial Boot to the Neck?

While Western governments may fret about China's growing influence in the region [Africa], some Chinese analysts see a measure of irony in the country's new role. Back in the 1960s and 1970s, China was more interested in world-wide revolution, third-world solidarity, and the backing of African liberation movements. Now, according to one scholar at the Chinese

Academy of Social Sciences, China's behavior has more in common with that of the colonizers. "Since we are mainly there to make money and get hold of their resources," he says, "it's hard to see the difference."

—*The Economist*

Just as it was in the 1960s and 1970s, one of China's most powerful instruments of influence in Africa continues to be its heavily government-subsidized weapons of mass construction. The imperialistic difference now is the close and obvious ties of this aid to China's resource exploitation.

In the copper-rich Congo and oil- and timber-rich Equatorial Guinea, China is laying down the roads needed to move the resources to port cities for shipment to China. In Algeria, which has the fifth-largest natural gas reserves in the world, China is building everything from airport terminals and five-star hotels to nuclear reactors.

Rwanda, which is rich in gold, tin, and tungsten, has been on the receiving end of everything from roads and railways to convention centers and government buildings. In diamond- and gold-rich Sierra Leone, China has built a new parliament building, stadium, and government office buildings, along with tractor and sugar plants and the country's biggest hotel, while helping strategically located Ethiopia build Africa's largest dam.

Meanwhile, as noted in the *Wall Street Journal*, even in the tiny African Kingdom of Lesotho, "Chinese businessmen own and operate nearly half of all the supermarkets and a handful of textile companies." Chinese businesses also run major timber operations across the continent. Africa's largest timber producer, Gabon, is China's major African supplier, and China has emerged as the largest consumer of African timber.

What's wrong with this picture? China's brutal mistreatment of Zambian miners provides at least one answer to that question.

Shooting to Kill

Deep in the tunnel of the Collum mine, coal dust swirls thickly, and it's stifling for workers such as Chengo Nguni. He describes his $2-a-day job with a sigh: His supervisor yells incomprehensibly in Chinese. His rubber boots leak. The buttons to control the flow of ore out of the mine often deliver an electric shock. But the worst thing about life in the Chinese-owned mine in southern Zambia is that there is no such thing as a day off. Ever.

—Los Angeles Times

"The Chinese, they don't even consider us to be human beings," complains Albert Mwanaumo, a former Chambishi [copper] miner who said he was shot by a Chinese supervisor. "They think they have the right to rule us."

—Wall Street Journal

Zambia is the world's seventh-largest copper producer, and, illustrating China's penchant for locking down natural resources for its exclusive use, a Chinese company is now the proud owner of one of Zambia's largest copper mines, the Chambishi. China bought the shuttered Chambishi copper mine for the bargain price of $20 million, and then poured another $100 million of investment into the mine to quickly ramp up its copper production. Unfortunately, while China brought abundant new technology to the mining operation, it also imported its own brand of Dickensian slave-labor working conditions.

From the outset, all union activity was banned at the Chambishi, and anyone found engaging in such activity was immediately fired. Men were then often forced to work underground with neither boots nor safety gear. For all this, Chambishi's copper miners were paid less than even the meager minimum wage required by the Zambian government.

These deplorable working conditions would not have been exposed if it were not for an explosion at the site that killed 46 of the Zambian employees. This tragic accident generated a wave of anti-Chinese sentiment in Zambia because just before the explosion, the site's Chinese managers were seen rapidly driving away, saving their own skins while failing to warn the Zambian workers.

A subsequent investigation of the accident would later determine that lack of labor union oversight was a key contributing factor to the accident. This finding, and rising anti-Chinese sentiment, forced the Chinese to sign a collective bargaining agreement that promised both safer working conditions and the awarding of back pay. However, after the Chinese signed this collective bargaining agreement, they still failed to provide the back pay. The result was a worker protest that ended violently when a Chinese supervisor unloaded a shotgun blast into the crowd.

This Zambia case illustrates how China is ruthlessly exporting its own slave-labor working conditions to the African continent. China's forays into South Africa illustrate much more broadly how tight the Panda's hug can be—not just around a country's raw materials, but also around its *retail markets*, with a devastating effect on the domestic job base and wages.

The Plunder of South Africa

> Over the past year, South African clothing manufacturers have lost one-third of their market share, shedding some 17,000 jobs in the process. Thousands more jobs are on the line as Chinese imports of clothing, textiles, and footwear flood into the South African market.
>
> —Business Africa

South Africa's mineral wealth is absolutely staggering, and it is arguably the richest of the African nations. Besides being home to more than half of the world's gold reserves, South Africa possesses more than three-fourths of the world's manganese and almost three-fourths of the world's chromium. Both are essential in the alloying process for steel and other metals. South Africa is also home to more than half the world's platinum group metals, which are critical in auto production, and almost half of its vanadium, which is essential in the production of aerospace titanium alloys.

One would think that with such an embarrassment of mineral riches South Africa would run substantial trade surpluses with virtually all of its trading partners. Not so with China.

In fact, South Africa's exports to China have more than doubled in five years, but the trade has been largely in raw materials rather than manufactured goods. During this time, Chinese exports have taken a heavy toll on South Africa's textile and clothing industries. More broadly, the punishing effects of the China Price and China's unfair trading practices are now reaching deep into the poorest pockets of poverty as garment workers from Mozambique, Swaziland, and Uganda, as well as South Africa, are being pushed onto the unemployment line.

Moeletsi Mbeki, the deputy chairman of the South African Institute of International Affairs, has aptly described this imperialistic relationship: "We sell them raw materials, and they sell us manufactured goods with a predictable result—an unfavorable trade balance against South Africa."

Zimbabwe's Tobacco Road to Poverty

Zimbabwe doesn't have oil, but it is the world's second-largest exporter of platinum, a key import for China's auto industry. Chinese radio-jamming devices block Zimbabwe's dissident broadcasts, and Chinese workers built [President Robert] Mugabe's new $9 million home, featuring a blue-tiled roof donated by the Chinese government. While Western politicians railed against Mugabe last year for flattening entire *shantytowns, China was supplying him with fighter jets and troop carriers worth about $240 million in exchange for imports of gold and tobacco.*

—*Fortune*

The case of Zimbabwe likewise illustrates that it is not just minerals, metals, and raw materials that China is gaining control of in Africa, but also agricultural products. In the past, Zimbabwe sold its tobacco at an international auction for top dollar. However, as noted by Lindsay Hilsum, "Now the auction houses in Harare are silent—tobacco goes directly to China's 300 million smokers, as payment in kind for loans and investment from Chinese banks to Zimbabwe's bankrupt state-run companies. As Zimbabwe's agricultural sector collapses, the Chinese are taking over land that the Zimbabwean government confiscated from white farmers and cultivating the crops they need."

Much more broadly, China's agro-imperialism in Zimbabwe graphically illustrates once again how China's amoral foreign policies are helping to prop up dictators and rogue regimes around the world. Zimbabwe itself is a country ruled with an iron fist by President Robert Mugabe and, like Angola, which was discussed in Chapter 4, "The 'Blood and Nukes for Oil' Wars—The Sum of All Chinese Fears," it is a country whose vast mineral riches are being systematically looted by its ruling elites. As noted in the passage above from *Fortune* magazine, this looting would not be possible without the active economic and military assistance of the Chinese, for it is Chinese arms that keep Mugabe in power—even as Zimbabwe becomes the basket case of the world.

❖   ❖   ❖   ❖   ❖

The problems described above in the Congo, Lesotho, South Africa, Zambia, and Zimbabwe are just the tip of a much larger iceberg that is rapidly sinking the African continent into a deeper abyss of chronic poverty among the masses and unimaginable corruption among the elites. No one has described this problem better than South Africa's Mbeki:

> The political elite uses its control of the state to extract savings from the rural poor who, if they could, would have invested those savings either in improving their skills or in other productive economic activities. The elite diverts these savings towards its own consumption, and to strengthen the state's repressive instruments. Much of what Africa's elite consumes is imported. So state consumption does not create a significant market for African producers. Instead, it is a major drain on national savings that might have gone into productive investment. This explains Africa's growing impoverishment. The more the political elite consolidates its power, the stronger its hold over the state, and therefore the more rural societies sink into poverty and the more African economies regress.

Still, the African continent is hardly the only area of the world where Chinese imperialism is on the prowl for metals, minerals, raw materials, and agricultural resources. As it turns out, Latin America is providing China with equally target rich opportunities.

Indeed, the world's largest copper reserves are in Chile. Bolivia has the second-largest natural gas reserves in South America and is rich in cassiterite, the chief source of tin. Both Argentina and Brazil play host to large iron ore reserves. Even Cuba, most known for its sugar, is an important player in the mining market, with the world's fourth-largest nickel reserves and the sixth-largest cobalt reserves. In addition, on the wings of Chinese demand and financial capital, Paraguay, Brazil, and Argentina have become the world's major areas for new soybean cultivation.

China's Latin American Tangos

In the 1960s, the Soviet Union defied America's Monroe Doctrine by supporting Fidel Castro's military buildup in Cuba. Later, it supported insurgencies in Central America.

This triggered a competition among existing right-wing dicta-
torships, Marxist authoritarianism, and the U.S. democratic
model. In the end, democracy and open markets won.
Promoted by the United States, these principles have gener-
ally made Latin American states more viable politically, eco-
nomically, and commercially.

Today, another communist state—the People's Republic of
China (PRC)—is seeking trade, diplomatic, and military ties
in Latin America and the Caribbean. The region is rich in
natural resources and developing markets for manufactured
goods and even arms.

—Stephen Johnson, The Heritage Foundation

The Monroe Doctrine, which dates back to 1823, asserts the right
of the United States to prevent foreign powers from colonizing any of
the nations of Latin America. In challenging the Monroe Doctrine,
China is now employing many of the same imperial-colonial tricks in
the Americas that it has used so successfully in Africa.

For example, as noted in *The Economist,* many of the agreements
that China is entering into with Latin American nations "are loans for
the expansion of the infrastructure such as ports and railroads." Such
investments are squarely "focused on getting resources out of the
region."

Consider China's Chilean copper connection. Chile is the world's
biggest copper producer; China is the world's biggest copper consumer; and now, more than half of Chilean copper is shipped to
China out of ports that China has helped to expand and modernize.
As a quid pro quo for this copper trade, China has coaxed Chile into
signing free trade agreements that will effectively kill the ability of
indigenous industries to prosper. As noted by *The Economist,* "The
problem with supplying China with resources is that countries in the
Americas are missing out on the manufacturing or processing work
that could keep more wealth in the local economies."

Brazil is finding itself increasingly in a similar imperialistic squeeze as China ties its economic assistance to claims on Brazilian natural resources and access to Brazilian markets. Says Brazilian economist Roberto Giannetti da Fonseca on China's assistance; "China is 'not a strategic partner.' It merely wants to buy raw materials with no value added and to export consumer goods." Statistics from *The Economist* back up this claim as "nearly 60% of Brazil's exports to China are primary goods, largely soya and iron ore. Imports from China are more high-tech and varied, with electronics, machines, and chemicals in the lead. Now China is making inroads into such labor-intensive sectors as textiles, shoes, and toys, too."

Perhaps most troublesome of all of China's Latin America tangos is its increasingly close relations with Fidel Castro's Cuba. As I explain in more detail in Chapter 11, "Racing for the Ultimate Strategic High Ground—The Coming China Star Wars," China has taken over the Cuban military, port, and electronic and satellite spying facilities once used by the Soviet Union at the height of the Cold War. Cuba is, however, not just a strategic prize and listening post. Cuba is also home to some of the largest reserves of one of the world's most versatile metals: nickel. This is a metal used in everything from coins and magnets to alloys with steel, copper, aluminum, and gold. As the United States has tried to embargo nickel exports from Castro's Cuba to the West, this has merely allowed China to move closer to cornering the market on Cuban nickel.

Imperialism with a Taiwanese Twist—And Spies R Us

Two final observations on China's imperial strategy must be noted as this chapter ends. First, in both Latin America and Africa, China is pursuing its imperialistic agenda with a Taiwanese twist. Both Africa and Latin America are playing an ever-increasingly important role in Beijing's strategy of the "diplomatic encirclement" of Taiwan.

For example, as reported by Reuters, after Beijing announced cancellation of almost $20 million worth of debt and offered close to $4 million for the construction of critically needed roads, hospitals, and other infrastructure, Senegal broke off relations with Taiwan. Liberia similarly abandoned Taiwan after Beijing ponied up $25 million in reconstruction funds and a $5 million interest-free loan.

More broadly, almost half of the remaining 25 countries that now diplomatically recognize Taiwan are in Latin America, and China is aiming to pick off each of them with promises of lavish aid. One of the first defectors since the onslaught of China's Latin America offensive was the tiny island of Grenada. It offers a stark lesson in not only Beijing's "dollar diplomacy" but also the personal and sometimes quite penny ante politics of corruption.

The triggering event for Grenada cutting Taiwan loose was China's donation of $50,000 to a hurricane relief fund. As reported in the *Taiwan Times,* this money promptly found its way not into Red Cross coffers where it was supposed to go but rather into the "pockets of Grenadian Prime Minister Keith Mitchell's government." Of course, it did not hurt the cause of severing Taiwanese ties that Beijing had already pledged $100 million in aid over a 10-year period. "The tiny Caribbean island of Dominica made a similar switch in March 2004 after China promised it $100 million in aid over five years, more than $1,400 for each of the island's 70,000 people."

Second, as indicated by our earlier discussion of Cuba, China often intertwines its longer-range military and strategic objectives with its imperialistic economic goals. The dangers inherent in China's ongoing evisceration of the Monroe Doctrine are reflected in this cautionary tale and closing passage from the *Miami Herald:*

> The strategic equation in our own hemisphere is changing like a cancer that you can't feel. ... At tracking stations in Brazil, Chinese technicians familiarize themselves with new digital reconnaissance equipment that might someday enable them

to stalk and destroy U.S. intelligence satellites. In computerized listening posts in Cuba, Chinese experts in electronic espionage scoop up signals from U.S. military satellites and sift through the contents of millions of American telephone conversations for intelligence. At airfields in Venezuela, Chinese military officers instruct pilots in the fine points of new transport planes that the government of President Hugo Chávez has purchased from Beijing. From this toehold, China hopes to expand military sales—eventually including jet fighters—throughout South America. ... Because China's initiative in the Western Hemisphere has involved tiny nibbles rather than a single bold thrust, it has attracted little public attention. But that doesn't make it any less real.

6

The Global Warming Wars— Killing Us (and Them) Softly with Their Coal

China's population is so big and its resources so scarce that if we continue to ignore our environmental problems, that will bring disaster for us and the world.

—Pan Yue, China's Environmental Protection Administration

As an example of the severity of China's self-inflicted air pollution crisis, it would hard to top the northeast city of Benxi—one of the 20 largest cities in China. At one point, this heavy industry center, which burns roughly seven million tons of coal per year and produces more steel per capita than any other city in China, literally disappeared from satellite images because of the dense cloud of haze and soot that enveloped it.

The obvious question for those of us living outside China is this: Why should we care? Indeed, if one were to view the heavily polluted Chinese landscape from a totally free-market perspective, one might arrive at this conclusion: If the Chinese want to pollute their air and water so consumers in other countries are thereby able to enjoy lower-priced products, so be it.

One problem with this way of thinking—aside from its obvious disregard for the hundreds of millions of innocent Chinese victims of pollution—is this: As you saw in Chapter 1, "The Cheating 'China Price' and Weapons of Mass Production," China's extremely lax environmental regulations and weak enforcement allow Chinese manufacturers to produce at an unfair cost advantage over competitors. China's wanton fouling of its air and water thus represents an important source of competitive economic advantage that is helping to depress wages and put millions of people out of work in other countries.

There is, however, an arguably even bigger problem with China's pollution that affects literally everyone on the planet. China's prodigious pollution is now spewing well beyond its environmentally porous borders.

Some of China's environmental fallout is *regional*. Much of the acid rain now falling on the forests, farmland, and rice fields of Japan, the Korean Peninsula, and Taiwan originates in China. "Chinese-made" acid rain is so bad that it approaches levels of acidity equal to that of vinegar.

In addition, Japan, Korea, and Taiwan are now regularly pummelled by fierce sandstorms that deposit tons upon tons of toxic yellow dust across these neighboring lands. These dust storms first rise up in China's Gobi Desert, suck up all manner of toxic pollutants as they pass over China's industrial heartland, and then quite literally sandblast China's neighbors.

In addition to these regional environmental effects, China's pollution, like its mercantilist economy, has also gone *global*. One problem is a particularly virulent brand of Chinese smog or "chog." This chog is sucked up into the jet stream and then travels as far away as Canada and the United States. Indeed, at times, as much as 25% of the air pollution in cities like Los Angeles and San Francisco originates in China.

There is also what may turn out to be the mother of all global environmental issues—global warming. You may not be surprised to know that China has now surpassed the United States as the world's biggest global warmer. What is truly astonishing, however, is that within 25 years, China's carbon dioxide emissions will be double that of all other industrial nations combined!

The irony of China's prolific global warming contributions is that of all the large nations on Earth, China may well have the most to lose. Global warming threatens to melt the glaciers in the Tibetan Plateau that feed China's major rivers—the Yellow and Yangtze. Rising sea waters from the melting of the polar ice caps likewise threaten to flood coastal cities such as Shenzhen and Shanghai, along with much of coastal China, where the bulk of China's manufacturing might is concentrated. In addition, prolonged drought in China's northern breadbasket, which is already facing a severe water shortage, is projected to dramatically cut China's ability to feed itself.

In the analysis that follows, two things should become readily apparent. First, the scope of China's environmental degradation is quite literally breathtaking. Second, and even more disturbing, China is not really making a "choice" to be one of the world's worst polluters. Rather, like the toxic yellow dust storms being swept along the jet stream dispersing around the world and Chinese chog, the Chinese people are being swept along by a complex set of political factors and a model of unsustainable economic development that can only end badly—not just for the hundreds of thousands of Chinese dying annually from air pollution-related diseases, but for all of us—unless something is done now.

You Can't Tell Your Worst Polluter without a Scorecard

The Middle Kingdom [China] is hurtling toward environmental catastrophe—and perhaps an ensuing political upheaval. Already, most Chinese cities make Los Angeles look like a Swiss village.

—Joshua Kurlantzick, *The New Republic*

When an American hockey player suffered symptoms from
mercury contamination, he never expected that he might have
power plants half way across the world in China to blame.

—*Yale Global Online*

Any discussion of the China Air-Pollution Wars must start with
the most salient statistics. Here, then, is China's horrific air-quality
scorecard as compiled by respected bodies such as the World Bank
and China's own Environmental Protection Administration:

- China is home to 16 of the 20 most polluted cities in the world.
- Of China's 100 cities with more than a million people each,
  fully two-thirds fail to meet World Health Organization air-
  quality standards.
- China is the world leader in sulfur dioxide emissions—the primary culprit responsible for smog. China's highly toxic smog, or
  "chog," not only reduces visibility, it also kills by attacking both
  the heart and lungs.
- China releases 600 tons of mercury into the air annually, nearly
  a fourth of the world's non-natural emissions. Mercury destroys
  the nervous system. Children are particularly vulnerable to
  symptoms ranging from rashes, spasticity, and convulsions to
  the loss of hair, teeth, and nails—the term "Mad as a Hatter"
  comes from the use of mercury in hat making.
- China is the world leader in generating ozone-depleting substances. Loss of the world's ozone layer increases cancer risks,
  harms plant and marine life, helps melt the polar ice caps, and
  contributes to rising sea levels and coastal flooding.

The World Bank estimates that pollution costs China between
8% and 12% of its more than $1 trillion gross domestic product
(GDP) every year. These costs include increased medical bills, lost
work due to illness, damage to fish and crops, and money spent on
disaster relief.

In a study conducted jointly with the Chinese government, the
World Bank has also determined that air pollution kills a staggering

number of Chinese every year—some 700,000 souls. What is perhaps most interesting about this study is that, in typical totalitarian big foot fashion, the Chinese government demanded that this statistic on Chinese deaths be suppressed in the printed edition of the World Bank's final report. Like China's pollution, that statistic has, however, been impossible to hide.

The World's Biggest Pollution Factory

The coal that has powered China's economic growth...is also choking its people.

—Elizabeth C. Economy

At the root of many of China's air-quality problems is its heavy dependence on relatively high-sulfur, low-quality coal for everything from electricity generation and industrial production to cooking and space heating in the home. China relies on coal for almost 75% of its energy needs. In fact, each year, China consumes more coal than Japan, the United Kingdom, and the United States combined.

The scale and scope of China's coal power plant construction program is almost beyond one's imagination. Consider that every single week, China adds one new large coal power plant to its energy base. Every single year, China builds enough new coal plants to light up the entire British Isles. In any given year, the amount of coal-fired capacity that China is building amounts to more than double that of the entire electricity-generating capacity of the state of California—more than 100 gigawatts. That China's coal appetites are voracious is aptly captured in this passage from the *Wall Street Journal*:

> On a recent hazy morning in eastern China, the Wuhu Shaoda power company revved up its production of electricity, burning a ton and a half of coal per minute to satisfy more than half the demand of Wuhu, an industrial city of two million people.

It's not just the quantity of coal used by China that matters. The large amount of coal in China's "energy mix" is quite different from virtually all the other major economies of the world, which depend much more on oil. China's heavy coal dependence, coupled with a woeful lack of pollution-control technologies, make China's air-quality problem a very different one from that of developed countries, such as the United States and Germany, in at least three ways:

First, unlike in the United States, Germany, or Japan where sophisticated pollution-control technologies are deployed, much of what Chinese power plants and factories spew in the air is not just sulfur dioxide but also a high percentage of fine particulate matter. This is a critical observation because particulate matter is the most damaging form of airborne pollutants.

Second, small cities in China are no better off than large cities in terms of ambient air quality. This is because small cities are as likely as large cities to depend on coal in both their residential and commercial sectors. That means that China's pollution woes are spread over the entire country in cities small and large rather than concentrated in a few large industrial hubs.

Third, unlike the developed world where the automobile is the single largest source of air pollution, China's current problem is primarily a "stationary source" one. These stationary sources range from large coal-fired power plants in huge factory towns to small coal-fired stoves and heaters in peasant homes.

The nightmare here is that even if China is able to get better pollution controls on its power plants, and even if it is able to convert some of its population to natural gas cooking, China's air basins are still likely to be overwhelmed in the next several decades by an explosion in the number of new vehicles on Chinese roads. Just consider this astonishing statistic reported by Elizabeth C. Economy: China is now adding 15,000 new cars *a day* to its roads, and it expects to have more cars than the United States—as many as 130 million—as early as 2040. In addition, Elizabeth C. Economy also reports the following:

First, China is expected to construct fully half of all the buildings in the world over the next 25 years. Beyond sheer quantity, the nightmare here is that these buildings will be electricity sinkholes because Chinese buildings are notoriously energy inefficient. This will only further exacerbate China's coal dependence and collaterally gargantuan pollution emissions.

Second, China plans to move almost a half a billion peasants off the farm into factories and cities over the next several decades. As a rule, urbanites introduced to the magic of refrigerators, TVs, and toasters use more than three times the amount of energy as their rural counterparts.

On top of all this, Chinese manufacturers are extremely energy inefficient. To produce an equivalent amount of goods, they use six times more resources than the United States, seven times more resources than Japan, and, most embarrassingly, three times more resources than India, to which China is most frequently compared. If ever there were a blueprint for a global pollution factory, China would be the model.

China's Long Arm Reach of Acid Rain

Walking in the rain in Taiwan might not be as romantic as it is in the movies, especially in winter, when a northeasterly wind starts to blow. Last December, officials at the Central Weather Bureau found that several areas in northern Taiwan had been significantly affected by pollution. ... Bureau officials pointed to an extreme case of acidity recorded at 3.6 pH in value in Keelung. Bureau officials remind people to wear hats or use umbrellas to avoid going bald as a result of the acid rain, adding that the acidity of rain in Keelung was only slightly less acidic than vinegar.

—Taipei Times

By definition, acid rain is rain with a pH reading of less than 5.6 (where 7 is neutral). It occurs when the sulfur dioxide and nitrogen dioxide emissions from power plants burning fossil fuels react in the atmosphere with water, oxygen, and various chemicals to form sulfuric and nitric acids.

Why is acid rain so dangerous? Because it is a very efficient killer. Acid rain kills fish when it falls into lakes, rivers, and streams. It directly kills crops and damages soil and thereby substantially reduces harvests. It indirectly kills forests by weakening trees and making them more susceptible to diseases. Acid rain also reduces visibility and eats away at building materials, car paint, and roofing on houses—with the damages running into the billions of dollars annually.

Acid rain now falls over two-thirds of China's land mass. Most of this acid rain is caused by sulfur dioxide emissions from China's ubiquitous coal plants. However, China's steel industry and its belching coking plants also play a big role in the problem.

As noted earlier, it is not just China and its people who are suffering. Roughly half of Japan's acid rain and a smaller but significant fraction of Taiwan's and the Korean Peninsula's acid rain carries the "Made in China" label.

A Chinese Grapes of Wrath

The once green pastures of eastern Inner Mongolia [in China] lately resemble a scene from the American Dust Bowl of the 1930s. Sand storms emanating from these desertified grasslands have become an increasingly common irritant in Northern Chinese cities, and their effects have recently been felt as far away as Colorado.

—American Embassy in China

Say the word *desert*, and the first word that is likely to pop into your head might be Sahara or Mojave—certainly not China. In truth,

China is one of the most desert-plagued nations on Earth. Fully one-fourth of its land mass, primarily in the northwestern part of the country, is desiccated dust. Within another 20 years, some experts predict that almost 40 percent of China will have been ground into sand.

Turning China into desert is hardly new. The Chinese philosopher Mencius noted the problem as far back as 300 B.C., and even pinpointed the human causes of the problem, principally overcultivation and overgrazing.

What is both new and alarming is the accelerating speed with which this process is now taking place. According to the Chinese Academy of Forestry, between the 1950s and 1970s, China lost only about 600 square miles to desert. Today, as the desert has approached within 150 miles of Beijing, roughly 2,000 square miles of Chinese real estate are now being lost to desertification *every year*. That number continues to rise despite massive efforts by the central government to contain it.

As the speed of China's desertification has been accelerating, so, too, has the frequency and severity of associated sand and dust storms. Prior to the 1990s, these storms were relatively rare. Now, however, China is likely to experience more than 20 episodes a year, with at least half of China being affected. These storms have become so severe that they are literally devouring portions of the Great Wall in northwest China. Consider this ever-more typical scenario:

> It is spring, and the latest windstorm whips across the steppes of Inner Mongolia. These gale-force winds send vortices of sand and dust clouds high up into the air for a ride upon the jet stream. As this giant yellow swirl moves eastward toward Beijing, it passes over China's industrial heartland and sucks up all manner of other highly toxic pollutants—from carcinogenic dioxins and fine particulates spewed from coal plants to heavy metals such as cadmium, copper, lead, and mercury.

After dumping tons upon tons of this toxic yellow stew along a string of Chinese cities and towns, the swirl first makes a "stopover" in Japan and Korea. There, according to South Korea's Rural Development Agency, "a single storm can dump more than 8,000 tons of sand." The worst storms close airports, roads, shops, and schools. More broadly, according to the United Nations Environmental Program, the cost of these dust storms to the region's economy is regularly topping $6 billion a year.

China's tons of yellow dust are not merely sandblasting China's neighbors and weighing down the regional economy. These swirling toxic clouds continue at speeds of upward of 1,500 miles per day, to complete their 7,000-mile journey to North American skies to greet us as we walk out of our Wal-Marts and Targets with baskets full of cheap Chinese goods. As Professor Tom Cahill of the University of California-Davis has duly noted: "We're a small world. We're all breathing each other's effluent."

The World's Biggest Global Warmer

Within 80 years, 30 million people in China are going to be under sea because of global warming and rising sea levels. We know it is going to happen, so we must look at ways of how to protect the area.

—Dr. Peter Walker, International Federation of Red Cross and Red Crescent Societies

Greenhouse gases consist primarily of carbon dioxide, but also include methane, nitrous oxide, ozone, and water vapor. They have been the Earth's friend because they act like a "thermal blanket" to keep Earth at a livable temperature. When the sun's radiant energy beats down on the planet, the Earth, in turn, wants to radiate this energy back into space. Greenhouse gases help trap some of that energy and, thereby, keep some of the heat in.

This "greenhouse effect" occurs in much the same way you would observe in an actual greenhouse. Without this natural global warming, Earth's average temperature would be much lower than around 60 degrees Fahrenheit, which is quite hospitable for our species and all the other animal, marine, and plant life that help make up the global food chain.

The problem now, however, is that as greenhouse gases continue to pile up in the atmosphere, the Earth is rapidly heating up to temperatures above that which are safe. Consider that the 10 hottest years on the planet have all occurred in the past 15 years. This rise in the Earth's temperature is having all sorts of negative economic and ecological effects.

For starters, our polar ice caps are melting. In addition, both the snow cover in the northern hemisphere and floating ice in the Arctic Ocean have visibly decreased. At the same time, these higher temperatures are also melting glaciers around the world that are the sources of much of the world's drinking water.

As noted earlier, both the Yellow River and Yangtze River in China are fed by glaciers in the Tibetan highlands. These glaciers are now melting much more rapidly than in previous years. Unless global warming is reversed, the most likely scenario over the next several decades is ever-more severe floods in China—followed by an abrupt drying up of the rivers as the glaciers go dry.

In addition to threatening the world's water supplies, global warming is having a variety of other radical effects—flooding some areas and punishing other areas with land-baking droughts. The result has been increased wildfires and dust storms, more intense and frequent hurricanes in the United States and typhoons in China, and "killer heat waves" in Europe and India.

Although many nations are contributing to the global warming problem, China is both the world's biggest global warmer and one of its biggest potential victims. China faces a perilous future of coastal flooding, severe water shortages, and declining crop production if global warming continues on its current trend.

You would think that with so much at stake China would be at the front of the pack calling for solutions to global warming. It's just the opposite. At every turn, China has taken the opportunity to blame developed countries, such as the United States, Japan, and the nations of Europe for the problem, and China does indeed have a point. The United States in particular has lagged abysmally in its efforts to solve the global warming crisis. That said, China continues to stonewall on this issue; and, fearful of being held accountable for its growing role in the problem, China has even gone so far as to attack the U.N. Security Council for even debating the issue of climate change.

The Troubles with China's Environmental Destruction Agency

All countries suffer internal tugs of war over how to balance the short-term costs of improving environmental protection with the long-term costs of failing to do so. But China faces an additional burden. Its environmental problems stem as much from China's corrupt and undemocratic political system as from Beijing's continued focus on economic growth. Local officials and business leaders routinely—and with impunity— ignore environmental laws and regulations, abscond with environmental protection funds, and silence those who challenge them.

—Elizabeth C. Economy

Why has China allowed itself to become the black lungs, yellow dust bowl, and biggest global warmer of the planet? This is an important question because, at least on paper, China has a set of environmental regulations almost as tough as those of the United States. In practice, however, the laws are a total sham.

As a root source of the problem, China's Environmental Protection Administration (EPA) is woefully understaffed. Whereas the U.S. EPA employs close to 20,000 regulators, China's counterpart has only 300. In addition, China's local environmental bureaus most empowered to enforce the federal government's edicts are highly autonomous, far more concerned with gunning the local economy than protecting the environment, and often corrupt.

In a highly interrelated problem, many of China's worst polluters are also government-run enterprises. This raises an obvious "fox guarding the henhouse" issue because it requires the government to police itself.

There is also the very large matter of the exceedingly small fines that Chinese regulators typically impose on polluters. These fines are seen not as an effective deterrent but rather as a small cost of doing business.

The coup de grâce for China's environment is China's sordid historical relationship with the Earth. For centuries, the country's rulers have subjugated nature to their needs instead of attempting to live in harmony with it. As Chairman Mao once put it, man must "conquer nature and thus attain freedom from nature."

In the communist system, there is also precious little respect for the more diffuse rights of others to everything from clean air and water to human rights. That's why in this permissive atmosphere, it is routine for Chinese factory managers to either ignore environmental rules or, in some ways far worse, to engage in elaborate ruses to fool environmental inspectors.

One such ruse, which is practiced by as many as one-third of all large Chinese companies, is to switch on the company's pollution-control technologies only during government inspections. This is easy to accomplish because corrupt regulators often tip off the companies in advance of inspections in exchange for bribes. That's why Joseph Kahn of the *New York Times* has correctly noted the following:

> The enormous human and environmental toll of China's rapid development is not just an unintended side effect but also an explicit choice of business executives and officials who tolerate death and degradation as the inevitable price of progress.

Groups such as the Sierra Club are not likely to ride to the rescue either. Rather than being respected in China, environmentalists are subject to all manners of abuse—from fines and beatings to prison. A "poster child" for this problem is Wu Lihong. He went from being honored in the Great Hall of the People as one of China's top environmentalists to being beaten and jailed a year later on trumped-up charges of blackmail.

As a final cause of China's lack of environmental protection and enforcement, there is the meteoric rise of powerful foreign companies and their lobbyists in the political and economic fabric of China. As noted in Chapter 1, much of the foreign direct investment flooding into China comes from companies based in countries such as Japan, South Korea, Taiwan, and the United States that are actively exporting some of their most polluting industries to China. Indeed, it is precisely China's dysfunctional system of environmental protection that helps make China such a magnet for foreign investment.

There is both a danger and a paradox here that should not be lost on any student of Chinese history aware of the "foreign humiliation" that China was subjected to in the nineteenth and twentieth centuries. The danger is that these powerful foreign economic interests are overpowering the political will of the central government, thereby rendering it impossible for China to get a handle on its own pollution problems. The paradox is that as China's Communist Party seeks to mold the country into a superpower, it is quickly losing control of its own destiny to powerful foreign economic interests.

Add all of this up and you get what you got: the most heavily polluted country on the planet with enormous environmental problems that are not just local and regional, but global in scope.

7

The Damnable Dam and Water Wars—
Nary a (Clean) Drop to Drink

Zhang Lishan stands on a ridge of dirt tending a small vegetable garden surrounded by pools of stagnant, stinking water. His plot near the banks of the Yangtze River in China's eastern Anhui province is irrigated by the runoff from a large paper mill. "I can hardly grow anything because this water is poisoned," he says. "It kills all the fish and many of my neighbors have been made sick." At the point where the runoff meets the river, a dead pig bobs on the wake of a cargo ship steaming past. Mr. Zhang is far from alone in his distress. Across large swaths of China's rapidly industrializing countryside, polluted water is killing tens of thousands of people every year, threatening the health of millions more, and cutting the crop yields of farmers who have few other economic resources to fall back on.

—Financial Times

Of the 2000-plus villagers in Huang Meng Ying, nine are deaf, 14 mentally disabled, three blind, and nine physically handicapped. The villagers also point to the surge in birth defects, lesions, and gall bladder infections in recent years—a sure indication, they feel, that the water is contaminated. ... A glimpse of the river, which once irrigated what was one of the most fertile regions of the country, reveals why the villagers have arrived at this conclusion. The once-clear waters are today a floating mass of garbage and chemical effluents, unfit for irrigation, let alone drinking.

—Asian Chemical News

China is not just the world's "factory floor." It is now also the world's leading "cancer factory" and disease incubator. One major reason is a hellish level of water pollution almost beyond imagination.

Chinese water pollution is so severe that it has reduced many of China's lakes and many segments of its rivers to nothing more than turbid garbage bins and stinking, flourescent green dead zones literally toxic to the touch. As a result, over half of the population—some 700 million Chinese—now drink water well below World Health Organization standards while stomach, liver, and intestinal cancers have become one of the biggest "peasant killers" in the countryside.

China's River Styx brand of water pollution is caused not just by the massive dumping and indiscriminate burning of toxic wastes by heavy industry. An avalanche of excess fertilizer and pesticide runoff and a mountain of animal and human waste stand equally tall as culprits.

The Wages of Heavy Industry Is Death

China's government rushed Thursday to shield the country's southern business center, Guangzhou, from a toxic spill flowing toward the city of seven million—the second manmade disaster to hit a Chinese river in six weeks. As a slick of toxic benzene from the first accident in the north arrived in Russia, where worried residents flooded a telephone hot line, authorities in southern China were dumping water from reservoirs into the Bei River to dilute a cadmium spill from a smelter.

—Associated Press

China's worst-polluting industries include paper and pulp, food, chemicals, tanning, and mining. Just on the banks of the Yangtze River alone, there are more than 9,000 chemical plants and tens of thousands more polluters of all shapes and sizes.

In some cases, small factories without adequate pollution-control technology wantonly dump a toxic stew of wastes and chemicals into rivers and streams. In other cases, large factories equipped with the latest and most sophisticated pollution-control technologies simply do not use the technologies for fear of driving up production costs—and without any fear of sanctions by lax regulators and often complicit local officials.

The most common toxic pollutants being unleashed include dioxins, solvents, and PCBs; various metals such as mercury, lead, and copper; and highly persistent pesticides ranging from chlordane and mirex to DDT. As noted by the *Wall Street Journal:*

> The textile industry is one of China's dirtiest. In addition to heavy metals and various carcinogens, fabric dyes may contain high levels of organic materials, and thread is often dipped in starch before it is woven into the fabric. The breakdown of large amounts of organic compounds, such as starch, can suck all the oxygen out of a river, killing fish, and turning the water into a stagnant sludge.

China's waterways are not just turning fluorescent green from pond scum. They often run red, blue, or any one of a number of colors from the dyes regularly dumped from factories serving the most visible of multinational corporations—from the Gap, Tommy Hilfiger, and Reebok to Nike, Land's End, and Abercrombie and Fitch. Notes the *Wall Street Journal,* there's a joke in China today that "you can tell what colors are in fashion by looking at the rivers."

Letting a Thousand Algal Blooms Bloom

With increasing affluence, China's per capita consumption of meat, milk, and eggs increased fourfold, fourfold, and eightfold, respectively, between 1978 and 2002; its egg consumption now equals that of rich nations. This means more agricultural wastes, animal droppings, fish droppings, fish food, and fertilizer for aquaculture, tending to increase terrestrial and aquatic pollution.

—Professors Jianguo Liu and Jared Diamond

As the world's largest fertilizer user, China consumes more than 50 million metric tons annually. Due to peasant ignorance, the problem with this fertilizer use is widespread *overuse*. This reduces fertilizer efficiency and therefore requires ever larger applications to achieve a given yield. The result has been a new kind of "flooding" problem in China, that of excess fertilizer runoff flooding into China's rivers and streams.

With this runoff, fertilizer nutrients such as nitrogen and phosphates have triggered an explosion of so-called "algal blooms" in China's rivers and lakes as part of a broader process of *eutrophication*. This eutrophication process literally sucks the oxygen out of the water and kills all fish and plant life. The net result is an extremely foul-smelling and turbid dead body of water.

China is also the world's second-largest consumer of pesticides, and, as with fertilizers, overuse is rampant. Moreover, many of the pesticides used by Chinese farmers have been banned both in China and the rest of the world, including the very deadly DDT. As a result of this wanton use of pesticides, numerous scientific studies are now finding excessive pesticide residues across a wide range of Chinese products, from fruits and vegetables to mushrooms and Chinese teas. These toxic pesticides not only cause cancer; they can also trigger allergies, nervous system damage, birth defects, and the collapse of a person's immune system.

China's toxic agricultural products are not just killing the Chinese people. They are increasingly finding their way into the global food chain as China's food exports boom.

A Mount Everest of Sewage and Dangerous Viral Soup

Dongxing City is just one example of how 80 million people in Guangdong Province live close to the animals, poultry, and fish they eat. At a piggery close to Mrs. Yang's, a farmer keeps young chickens next to his pigs. All the piggeries empty their waste into the ponds where shrimp and grass-carp are raised for the table. In other places, battery chickens are kept above the pig pens, feeding their waste into the pigs' food troughs.

The close proximity and cross pollution adds to the risk of animal viruses infecting humans, either directly or via pigs. "It's a complete soup of chemicals and viruses," says Christine Loh, a former legislator.

—Sydney Morning Herald

China is the world's undisputed "emperor of pork." China's hog farmers produce 70% of all meat produced in China and 50% of all the pork produced in the world. The result is a mountain of piggery waste, much of which is regularly dumped, or seeps, into China's waterways. While these piggery wastes provide a rich source of fuel for the eutrophication process, so, too, does the untreated human waste pouring forth into Chinese waterways from the largest urban population in the world. Indeed, Chinese cities generate more than a *trillion* tons of sewage each year—with 90% of these municipal wastes going either untreated or failing to receive proper sewage treatment.

In addition, it is critical to note here that a very different and even more deadly kind of "pollution," with the very broadest international reach, results from the overflow of animal and human wastes. China has become the world's prime breeding ground for new and exotic strains of influenza and other viruses, including both the deadly SARS virus and avian flu. The primary reason, as the preceding excerpt indicates, is that so many different farm animals live in such close proximity to humans and other species. The resultant "cross pollution" creates a "soup of chemicals and viruses" that now threatens the world with the possibility of a pandemic in which tens of millions of people may die.

The Red (Tide) Menace

A toxic red tide has blanketed the equivalent of more than 1.3 million soccer fields of sea off eastern China, threatening marine and human life. The tide is caused by plankton reproducing itself in large quantities due to nutrients provided in part by sewage and industrial waste.

—Reuters

It is not just China's lakes, rivers, and streams that are being choked by a flood of pollutants. China's ocean waters are also suffering mightily from waves upon waves of toxic and organic pollutants and a growing epidemic of red tides. The problem is particularly acute in the relatively shallow Bohai Sea off northern China. This is one of the world's busiest waterways, and it is characterized by a very minimal tidal exchange, which makes it particularly susceptible to pollution. According to Elizabeth C. Economy, "China releases about 2.8 billion tons of contaminated water into the Bo Hai annually, and the content of heavy metal in the mud at the bottom of it is now 2000 times as high as China's own official safety standard."

More broadly, China's particularly virulent red tides are being ignited by the wholesale dumping of sewage, agricultural, and industrial pollution into ocean waters. These red tides are merely an ocean-going version of the eutrophication process now strangling China's fresh water resources.

China's red tides are destroying fish stocks and devastating other marine life that China and other countries in the region depend upon for food. What is perhaps most worrisome is the rapidly increasing frequency and intensity of China's red tide episodes. Indeed, China has seen an astonishing forty-fold increase in the incidence of red tides in just the past few years.

Nary a Drop to Drink

She gave birth to one of the world's most glorious ancient civilizations. For more than 4000 years, she has nurtured millions of fields and farmers spread alongside her. Millions still rely on her bounty today. But like so many working mothers, the Yellow River is exhausted, her resources dwindling, her energy flagging. The 3600-mile-long waterway known throughout history as "China's sorrow" because of a penchant for spilling over is now causing despair for precisely the opposite reason: It is drying up.

—*Los Angeles Times*

Much of China's fresh water in its rivers, lakes, streams, and wells is just too polluted to use in irrigation, much less for drinking. This horrific water pollution is thus exacerbating a water-scarcity problem that is already the worst among any of the larger economies of the world. In fact, China supports more than 20% of the world's population with just 7% of the world's water supplies.

China's most severe water-scarcity problems are being felt in its heavily populated North China Plain. This extremely fertile breadbasket possesses a little more than 20% of China's arable land but less than 4% of its water resources. It is through this fertile Northern Plain that China's "Mother River"—the Yellow River—runs.

Fifty years ago, the Yellow River ran bountifully to the sea. Today, however, as stark testimony to China's growing water-scarcity problems, the Yellow River can run dry for more than 200 days a year. For much of the year, the easternmost portions of the river turn into a highway, with cars and trucks traversing the dusty riverbed.

It is not just Chinese farmers suffering from an extreme lack of water. Almost half of China's 660 cities face water shortages, more than a hundred of which face extreme water shortages. Water is scarcest in some of China's most heavily populated and industrialized cities. Besides bone-dry Beijing and Shanghai, water-scarce areas include the key industrial provinces of Jiangsu, Hebei, Shanxi, Shandong, Tianjin, Henan, and Ningxia. These cities and provinces provide a lion's share of China's GDP; and in these areas, reduced flows of many of China's rivers are already significantly reducing the amount of hydroelectric power necessary to keep China's smelters, paper mills, petrochemical plants, and other factories humming.

That Giant Sucking Sound—China's Dangerous Game of Groundwater Extraction

The massive extraction of groundwater in the North China Plain has led to a rapid decline in the groundwater table. In agriculture, one of the consequences of groundwater depletion has been exhaustion and thus desertion of wells.

—Hong Yang and Alexander Zehnder

To slake its ever-growing thirst, China is aggressively "mining" many of its deepwater aquifers. This groundwater extraction is a dangerous game for at least four reasons.

First, the reliance on groundwater mining is unsustainable. Unlike shallower aquifers, which can be replenished by annual rainfall, the deepest aquifers are nonrenewable resources. Thus, any reliance on these aquifers for ordinary needs is taking place on borrowed time.

Second, as these groundwater aquifers are tapped, groundwater tables decline. That's why the water tables beneath much of northern China are shrinking by about five feet per year. This is forcing farmers to drill ever deeper and deeper wells, leading many lakes and streams to dry up.

Third, and most subtly, China's deepwater mining is inducing seawater contamination of its freshwater supplies. As fresh groundwater is sucked out of coastal aquifers, sea water seeps in and poisons wells and water supplies. This problem is particularly acute in the coastal areas of Dalian and Yantai. Here, more than 5,000 wells have been destroyed, production on 300,000 acres of irrigated farmland has been cut in half, and almost a million people and a quarter of a million livestock do not have enough water.

Finally, there is that sick, sinking feeling of subsidence now being felt by some of China's wealthiest cities. As Elizabeth C. Economy has noted, Shanghai and Tianjin have sunk by more than six feet during the past 15 years. In Beijing, which alone sucks out more than 200 million tons of subterranean water a year, subsidence has destroyed factories, buildings, and underground pipelines and is threatening the city's main international airport.

The Damnable Dam Wars

The sheer pointlessness of China's vast investment in dam building was brought home by the 1998 floods, which killed 4,000 people and cost the economy $36 billion. The dams have done nothing to stop the floods, which have been increasing in frequency and severity.

—*Asia Times*

You might think that a country facing a severe water shortage might not have to worry about flooding. In China's case, you'd be dead wrong. Whereas the North and West of China are parched, the more southern areas through which the mighty Yangtze River flows are highly prone to flooding. These flood-prone areas are home to about 50% of the total population and contribute two-thirds of both the total agricultural and industrial output.

To cope with its flooding and water-scarcity problems—as well as to help generate electricity for its mighty manufacturing economy— China has become the "dam happiest" country on Earth.

At more than 85,000 dams and counting, Chinese leaders boast of having the tallest dams, the largest by reservoir capacity, the dam with the highest ship lift, and the most powerful electricity producer. From arch dams, earthen dams, and gravity dams to cascade and concrete-faced rockfill dams, China has it all.

China should not be boasting about its dams, however. Instead, China's top leadership may well want to reconsider the perilous path it has chosen to take. For if ever there were a double-edged sword, a dam-happy strategy would be it.

On the beneficial edge of that sword, large dams generate significant amounts of cheap electricity. They store water when there is a surplus, for use in irrigation during times of scarcity. They protect arable land from flood and soil erosion. They can help promote aquaculture and fisheries development as well as tourism, recreation, and inland navigation. They can even change the local climate (for better *or* worse) by increasing humidity and precipitation.

On the other, much more dangerous edge of the sword, large dams often destroy the very waters they harness along with the agricultural lands they are trying to improve. Perhaps the worst aspect of large dams is their relatively short useful shelf life. As silt builds up behind a dam, the reservoir becomes shallower and shallower, so less electricity is generated, less water for irrigation is stored, and flood control becomes increasingly more difficult. Last, but hardly least, is the possibility of a catastrophic accident should a silted-up dam be breached and collapse, sending a roaring wave of water downriver on a devastating path of destruction.

The poster child for China's dam-happy strategy—and the extremely high risks this strategy entails—is China's highly controversial Three Gorges Dam.

The Three Gorges Meets the Three Stooges

China's showcase hydro-engineering project, the Three Gorges Dam, could become an environmental catastrophe unless remedial action is taken, the Chinese state media reported yesterday. In an unusually blunt public assessment, officials warned that landslides and pollution were among the "hidden dangers" facing the world's biggest hydro-electric plant. The alarmist reports, carried by the Xinhua news agency and the People's Daily website, were in stark contrast to the congratulatory tone of most previous domestic coverage of the project, which was planned for flood control along the Yangtze and for lessening China's dependence on power driven by coal.

—London Guardian

The Three Gorges Dam is the largest hydro-electric plant on the planet. It is also the world's biggest environmental catastrophe in the making. This most damnable of dams was fiercely opposed by scientists and environmentalists both within and outside of China. However, the Three Gorges Dam has been rammed down the throat of the Chinese people by a government that now has a disaster on its hands potentially far worse than even the dam's many critics warned of.

The "Three Gorges" literally comprise a series of canyons along a particularly treacherous portion of China's Yangtze River downriver from one of China's largest industrialized cities, Chongqing. Prior to

the dam's construction, swift currents and hidden rocks made navigation particularly treacherous through the Three Gorges, and one
important purpose of the dam has been to tame this wild stretch so
that ships as large as 10,000-ton freighters can make the trip down the
river toward Shanghai.

Improved navigability of the Yangtze is hardly the only, or the
most important, goal of the Three Gorges Dam. The project was also
built to control the floods that regularly threaten the millions of
people living along the banks of the Yangtze and to provide cheap
hydroelectric power for China's mighty manufacturing machine.

Today, China's "Great Wall on the Yangtze" stands more than 600
feet tall, is almost 400 feet wide at the bottom, and stretches almost a
mile and a half across the river. What is most impressive, and potentially the most dangerous fact about the dam, is not its height and
width, but rather the mammoth reservoir that the dam has created.
This is a reservoir that is 400 miles long and 70 miles wide and holds
five trillion gallons of water—equal to one-fifth of all the freshwater
consumed in the United States annually.

Before filling this reservoir, the Chinese government had to relocate almost 1.5 million people. In fact, submerged beneath the surface of this reservoir are two Chinese cities, 11 Chinese counties, 116
towns, and 4,500 villages. Another aspect of the fierce political con-
troversy surrounding the dam has been the loss of an abundance of
archaeological and historical artifacts. In addition, there are more
than 1,500 submerged factories—many with the capability of releas-
ing all manner of toxins into the waters of the Yangtze.

At least for now, the Three Gorges Dam is delivering on its promise to provide an important new source of electricity for China. Over
time, however, massive silt buildup behind the dam threatens to significantly cut the dam's electricity output, which is the Achilles heel
of all large dam projects. Meanwhile, the myriad of other problems
spawned by the dam threaten to spin out of control. As one surprised

government official has put it, "We thought of all possible issues, but the problems are all more serious than we expected."

One such problem that graphically illustrates the law of unintended consequences is this: Although the Three Gorges Dam was supposed to control flooding, it is now actually *increasing* flood risk. Because the river now flows with much less silt, it also flows much faster. This faster-flowing river is, in turn, putting much more force on a set of dikes that have been built over the centuries to contain the river. The very real threat now is that some of these dikes will be gouged out by the rushing water, collapse, and unleash a flood of water onto the cities and towns downstream.

Reduced silt flow downstream has also spawned another unintended consequence. Less silt now means the Chinese sunshine can penetrate deeper into the river. This increased sunlight is, in turn, accelerating the growth of photosynthetic algae and significantly adding to the epidemic of large-scale algal blooms across Chinese waterways.

It is not just the waters downstream from the Three Gorges Dam that are suffering. The dam's reservoir itself is slowly, but inexorably, turning into a toxic, turbid stew as it traps more and more pollutants, sewage, and garbage behind its "Great Wall."

Still, a third unintended consequence of the dam is a rapid increase in the number of landslides. The land along the riverbanks, once high and dry, is now being waterlogged and loosened up by the reservoir. This, coupled with the enormous pressure of the water in the reservoir itself, is triggering landslides that have already produced waves over 150 feet tall that have dragged farmers to their deaths and drowned fishermen.

Because of the threat of such landslides, the government is being forced to relocate another three to four million Chinese people from the area. Adding to the intense political turmoil surrounding these forced locations, some of these people will be "two-time migrants" who were part of the original evacuation prior to the dam's construction.

Beyond these horrific problems of increased flood risk, pollution, and landslides, the dam is killing fish by blocking fish migration and huge mounds of rubbish are piling up behind the dam.

In addition, two catastrophic scenarios hang heavy over the Three Gorges Dam. First, if silt continues to rapidly build up behind the dam, eventually the dam will not be able to contain a flood crest and will surely be breached. Second, the mass of water in the reservoir is so heavy that it may alter the pressure in the rocks below and induce an earthquake. With the dam itself built in the vicinity of several fault lines, this earthquake may, in turn, cause the dam to collapse. Such a collapse would unleash the biggest fresh water-based tsunami ever witnessed. The death toll would run into the millions; the economic costs would run into the billions; and the political and social havoc that would likely ensue might even bring down the government, which insisted on building the project to begin with.

Drums along the Mekong

From its origin in the high plateau of Tibet, the Mekong River is 2,800 miles long and the twelfth longest river in the world, flowing through six countries that include China, Burma, Thailand, Laos, Cambodia, and Vietnam. True to its name (Mekong means Mother River in Laotian), the Mekong River is the lifeline to more than 60 million inhabitants in downstream countries such as Laos, Thailand, Cambodia, and Vietnam. Most of them are poor fishermen living off the river fish catch or poor farmers using the river water and rich silt to grow rice. They also use the river as their principal means of transportation. The biggest threat to their livelihood is the hydro-electric dams built or planned by the Chinese in Yunnan Province. Even the survival of the river may be in serious doubt in the next few decades.

—Tran Tien Khanh

To end this chapter, it is critical to point out that China's dam-happy strategy is not just threatening Chinese citizens. China's upstream positioning on the Mekong River relative to its downstream neighbors, coupled with its overwhelming size and military might, put China in a position to dam the Mekong with bullying impunity.

China's grand Mekong River design will eventually include 15 large dams. The first two, the Manwan and Dachaoshan, were completed in 1993 and 2002, respectively. Together, they generate close to 3,000 megawatts of electricity—equivalent in output to about three large nuclear reactors.

It is the third dam now under construction, however, that most alarms China's neighbors. When the Xiaowan Dam is completed in 2013, it will be as tall as a 100-story building, rank as the tallest dam in the world, and generate more than 4,000 megawatts of power.

The problems that China's mega-dams on the Mekong are likely to create are vast and far-ranging. The two dams already built have begun to affect the seasonal flow of the river. From the Chinese perspective, this is a good thing because it allows them to run large ships along the Mekong year-round while at the same time preventing seasonal flooding. However, the downstream perspective differs decidedly.

To understand why, consider the likely impacts of China's dams on one of the world's most fascinating ecological treasures, the legendary Lake Tonle Sap in Cambodia. For much of the year, the lake is only a yard deep with a footprint of only a bit more than 1,000 square miles. During the rainy season, however, flow from the Mekong River helps deepen the lake to roughly 30 feet and increases the area of the lake more than fivefold. This turns Lake Tonle Sap into one of the best breeding grounds for fish in the world. This eloquent passage from London's *Independent* explains why this is so:

The waters carry fertile sediment, fish larvae, and fingerlings into the forest, which turns into a vast fecund nursery ground for fish—the source of one of the world's biggest inland fisheries. Here you will find the last of the Mekong catfish, the largest freshwater fish, which grows to three metres [ten feet] long and can weigh more than a cow. There's also the striped snakehead, which lives among tree roots and in lakes and swamps, and is known for its ability to slither overland between pools. Of greater value to millions of Cambodians is the fact that the flooded forest is also the breeding ground for the trey riel (Henicorhynchus siamensis), a sardine-like fish found in almost every net on the river.

As the forest slowly drains each autumn, the fattened fish migrate throughout the Mekong River system, where local fishermen, many living in floating villages, know almost to the hour when the fish will pass by. The peak moment of the annual flood on the Tonle Sap is precisely ten days before the January full moon.

The intensity of fishing on the Tonle Sap in particular is extraordinary. Nets stretch for miles around the edge of the flooded forest. And near Phnom Penh, small wicker "bags" lowered into the river can catch half a ton of fish in 20 minutes.

The obvious problem facing the Tonle Sap is that China's megadams will even out the flow of water and thereby prevent the world's most fertile natural fishery from realizing its full depth and breadth in the critical fish-breeding season. Already, fish catches have declined dramatically. In addition, the Mekong is now much more prone to rapid rises and falls as an upstream China regulates its own rivers, seemingly oblivious to the natural habitat and concerns of its downstream neighbors.

The nation most at risk from China's Mekong River dams may not be Cambodia but rather Vietnam—the "last stop" of the Mekong on its way to the South China Sea. If anyone thinks that the mighty

Mekong cannot go dry during certain periods of the year as it approaches Vietnam, remember that the once-mighty Yellow River in northern China now runs dry more than 200 days a year. Already, for the Mekong, the death knell has begun to sound. Government officials recently reported that the Mekong River had recorded its lowest level ever and that it was "flowing 'close to rock bottom'" near the end of its journey in Vietnam.

It may be useful to close here with the observation that Vietnam continues to maintain one of the largest armies in the world, in large part because of its historical enmity with China. Few people may remember that "other Vietnam war." This exceedingly bloody 1979 war occurred when China invaded Vietnam with tanks and about 90,000 troops in retaliation for Vietnam's pro-Soviet actions in Cambodia. In the space of *fewer than ten days* of fighting, estimates are that anywhere from 40,000 to more than 100,000 Chinese and Vietnamese troops were killed or wounded. These figures rival the entire number of American soldiers killed in battle during its more than *ten-year* war in Vietnam (about 52,000). Although the relationship between China and Vietnam is much better today, if the Mekong were truly to dry up because of China's dam strategy, conflict between the two countries would become inevitable.

8

China's Chaotic "Wars from Within"— The Dragon Comes Apart at the Seams

Predatory officials rob farmers of their lands, forcibly evict residents from their homes, and cover up extravagant abuses of power—typically embezzlement, but also rape and murder. These officials close their eyes to labor exploitation and condone or profit from criminal rackets, human trafficking, and illegal mining. There is even a term in Chinese for local officials who collude with criminal gangs: "black umbrellas." With no avenues to seek redress, China's citizens are abused and exploited on a shocking scale. The problems are not confined to small towns or rural areas: Recent prominent corruption cases include the police chief of Shenyang in Liaoning province, the party secretary of Shanghai, and the head of the national Food and Drug Administration.

—Nicholas Bequelin, Human Rights Watch

In glorifying the peasant revolution that brought him and his communist cadres to power, Mao Zedong once famously noted, "A single spark can start a prairie fire." In today's China, that single spark of Mao's day has now been replaced by a cascade of fireballs. Over the past decade, the number of protests, riots, and strikes in China has risen to nearly 100,000 annually. What is perhaps most alarming to the Chinese government about these emerging "wars from within" is the diversity of their causes and their broad geographic sweep.

Across the broad expanse of China, peasants with pitchforks are protesting illegal land seizures, forced evictions, a crushing tax burden, rampant government corruption, and the transformation of their once-idyllic lands into polluted cancer factories. China's workers are revolting over everything from slave-labor conditions and stolen wages to the most dangerous working conditions in the world. Tens of millions of castoff senior citizens are rising up against the loss of their pensions and the outrageous cost of health care. Meanwhile out in China's wild west, ethnic tensions are boiling over into armed conflict.

For all these reasons, none of *The Coming China Wars* outside China's borders are likely to be as sudden, wrenching, and violent as China's wars from within. What the Chinese government fears most is that any one of these increasingly intense domestic conflicts may spark a revolution that topples their teetering government and triggers a descent into chaos. Consider this small sampling of confrontations over the past several years:

- In a protest against excessive taxes, a peasant woman from the town of Xianqio in Guangdong Province on China's southern coast refuses to pay a bridge toll. After she is badly beaten, villagers surround the toll station and torch it. They are soon joined by a crowd numbering close to 30,000. A thousand police officers use tear gas to dispel the rioters, a man is crushed to death by a fire truck, seven firefighters are injured, and 17 people are arrested.

- In Xianyang City, in central China's Shaanxi Province, more than 6,000 workers strike after a textile factory is privatized; and the new owner seeks to fire and then rehire them as "inexperienced workers" at much lower wages without their accrued retirement or medical benefits.

- In the city of Chizhou, just 250 miles southwest of Shanghai, a student on a bicycle collides with the Toyota sedan of a wealthy businessman whose bodyguards callously kick and beat the student. Fueled by cell phones and instant messaging, this encounter mushrooms into a "rich versus poor" conflict involving more than 10,000 people. The Toyota and a police car are smashed, and a supermarket owned by another wealthy businessman is looted.

- A similar incident occurs in Wanzou City, a town near the Chongqing municipal area crammed with thousands of unemployed workers and a quarter of a million peasants dislocated by the Three Gorges Dam project. After a wealthy local government official assaults a lowly street porter, more than 10,000 people go on a rampage, looting government buildings and torching a police car.

- In Sichuan, a province as large as France and bordered by the Tibetan Plateau, tens of thousands of farmers in Hanyuan county clash with the People's Armed Police when their land is seized for a hydro-electric plant, and they are given what even a local official acknowledges is "compensation too low to accept."

- More than a thousand miles away in Henan Province in China's rustbelt heartland, a seething ethnic clash between Muslim Hui and Chinese Han peasants leave more than 100 dead after a bloody fight with farm tools.

Peasants with Pitchforks

In a very short time, several hundred million peasants will rise like a mighty storm, like a hurricane. They will sweep all the imperialists, warlords, corrupt officials, local tyrants, and evil gentry into their graves.

—Mao Zedong, 1927

Almost 60% of the Chinese population is involved in agriculture, the average farmer's yearly income is a mere $400, and the vast majority of peasant families have only very small plots on which to eke out a very tough living. Because of the more than half a *billion* peasants in China and the harsh conditions they face, no specter is more chilling to the central government in Beijing than a peasant-led rebellion.

Despite their fear of a peasant revolt, China's Communist Party leadership has done little to quell rising peasant tensions. Instead, myopic, venal, and often incompetent Communist Party bureaucrats and functionaries have done much to fuel peasant discontent through forced evictions, a crushing tax burden, rampant and flagrant corruption, and an utter disregard for the environment in which farmers must scratch out their meager livings.

Consider first that to make way for capitalist development and the manufacturing jobs it brings, the communist Chinese bureaucracy typically serves as the primary phalanx for land seizures. The problem in many cases is not the evictions per se to turn farmland into factories or even the horrific pollution that results from turning prime farmland into chemical factories or tanneries. Rather, it is the accompanying corruption and greed—what *The Economist* refers to as "the land grabs orchestrated by venal local officials, who turf people off the land so as to do lucrative deals with carpet-bagging developers." In far too many cases, local government officials are blatant double dippers. They accept bribes from the developers for executing the land seizure, and then siphon off the money that would otherwise be paid as compensation to those forced off their land.

For those peasants not yet driven off their land by the forces of development, there is yet another trigger for their discontent: the heavy tax burden imposed on the peasantry by local government officials. This onerous tax burden would be bad enough if the revenues were used to provide services to the taxpayers, but more often than not, these revenues are used to finance the extravagant lifestyles of local party officials.

While peasants break their backs in the hot fields, party officials ride around in limousines, enjoy lavish banquets, meet their mistresses in upscale hotels, and send their "Little Emperor" offspring abroad for schooling—all the while dissipating China's wealth. In fact, as much as $60 billion is siphoned off each year to offshore accounts.

Here, however, is the unkindest cut of all for China's beleaguered peasants. When they do rise up for any one of a number of reasons, they are just as likely to be smacked back down by rural gangsters who are often enlisted by local village or Communist Party officials to suppress dissent. For all these reasons, China's prairies are being lit up by a thousand sparks of peasant outrage.

A Worker's Revolt That Would Make Karl Marx Proud

China has ten million slaves. The definition of a slave is someone who is given work and food but no wages. That's what these people are.

—Professor Zhou Xiaozheng, People's University of China

China's factory workers are not only some of the hardest working and most disciplined in the world. They also are forced to toil in dangerous and oppressive working conditions not seen since the Dickensian nineteenth century.

The worst of the worst are China's coal mines, where thousands of miners die annually and tens of thousands more are severely injured. In these mines, peasants are routinely forced to sign what are derisively referred to as "life-and-death contracts" that revoke all legal claims and grant them a small lump-sum payment in the event of death or injury.

Meanwhile, in China's factories, large and small, thousands of workers are dismembered or killed on a monthly basis—literally ground up by machinery. Thousands more are exposed to lethal doses of chemicals or dust that, years later, will take their lives.

It is not just that working conditions can be horrific. In many cases, the wages that workers do earn are not even paid. This most typically happens to migrant laborers in China's cities who are ruthlessly exploited because of their second-class status. The amount of monies withheld by unscrupulous employers is staggering, running into the billions of dollars each year.

The problem is most acute in China's frenetic construction industry, where it is common practice to feed and house the migrant workers but withhold their wages. The tragedy here is that the construction industry is second only to mining in terms of health and safety risks. As in the coal mines, most construction workers are poor migrants, and their injuries and casualties typically go unreported.

This is hardly the only slave labor in China. In an economic arrangement that harks back to the days of the Maoist communes, many enterprises house their workers in dormitories, which effectively turn China's workers into either slaves or indentured servants. In some cases, bars on the windows prevent their escape. In other cases, the "bars" are purely economic because many workers are forced to sign labor contracts that effectively indenture their services to a company for a long period. If a worker breaks this contract, the worker will owe the company such a large sum of money that it would be impossible to pay it.

Of course, all the problems are compounded by the lack of any meaningful worker-protection laws, the outlawing of labor unions by the government, and the lack of enforcement of the few labor laws on the books. Is it any wonder that a seething rage in the Chinese workplace is spilling over into increasingly violent worker protests?

The Gray Dragons—Where Have All the Pensions Gone?

The number of retirees in China's cities will soar from 48.2 million last year to 70 million in 2010 and 100 million by 2020, according to the Ministry of Labor and Social Security.

Unlike the United States and Europe, which prospered before their elderly populations expanded, China is in danger of growing old before it gets rich.

—*USA Today*

Prior to the economic reforms that began in the 1970s, the centerpiece of China's economy was its "iron rice bowl" system. In this Marxist system, all state-owned enterprises guaranteed workers not just a livable wage, but also housing, health care, and pensions.

The iron rice bowl was modeled on the Soviet-style collectivization of industry and embraced by Mao Zedong and the Communist Party shortly after their rise to power in 1949. The big problem with the iron rice bowl system, however, was that with their wages, benefits, and pensions guaranteed, Chinese workers had very little incentive to produce.

In the 1990s, the Chinese government began to rapidly dismantle its highly inefficient iron rice bowl system in favor of free-market enterprises. This "privatization" of China's industry, together with China's potent array of unfair trade practices, would soon make Chinese industry competitive with the rest of the world. However, China's shattering of the iron rice bowl has also left hundreds of millions of Chinese workers approaching retirement without the prospects of either an adequate pension or health care.

This is all a bitter, bitter irony for many loyal communists who stoically endured the ravages of both the Great Leap Forward and the Cultural Revolution. After all, for much of their life, they worked commune style for modest wages under what they thought was an ironclad Maoist social contract that they would have lifetime security. Now, the Communist Party has abandoned these senior citizens at the most difficult time in their lives, and their rage continues to build as the reality of a shredded "safety net" hits with full force.

China's Pay Up or Die Health-Care System

"Some 2,000 people mobbed and ransacked a hospital in southwestern China on Friday in a dispute over medical fees and shoddy health care practices," a human rights group said today. At least ten people were injured when police broke up the demonstration at Guang'an City No. 2 People's Hospital, according to the Hong Kong-based Information Center for Human Rights and Democracy. The area was described as under tight police control today, with at least five people detained on suspicion of instigating a riot. The unrest erupted after a three-year-old boy died in the hospital, where he had been rushed for emergency treatment for ingesting pesticides.... The human rights group said that essential medical care was denied the boy until his grandfather, who was taking care of him, could pay for the treatment. The boy died after the grandfather left to raise money. ... Medical costs are an enormously sensitive issue for tens of millions of people in Chinese cities and hundreds of millions in the countryside who have no medical insurance and no public safety net to cover soaring health care costs.

—New York Times

As bad as China's pension crisis may be, its health-care problems may be worse. China spends only 6% of its GDP on health care. This compares to 8% percent in Japan and fully 14% in the United States.

In today's China, there is an extreme shortage of doctors, and sick people are forced to pay for their health care upfront. Those lacking the means to pay are cast out of hospitals and left to die an often slow and painful death. A big part of the problem is the cost of medical insurance—$50 to $200 per year—in a country where the annual per-capita income for the vast majority of the population remains well below $1,000.

The rot in China's health-care system truly runs deep. Under China's privatized model of medicine, hospitals, pharmacies, and even doctors have been turned into "profit centers" expected to finance their activities through patient fees. The basic economic result has hardly been surprising: Hospitals and pharmacies ruthlessly mark up the prices of medicines by as much as 20 times their cost. Doctors then radically overprescribe drugs and get their kickbacks from these hospitals and pharmacies. As a result, more than half of what Chinese patients pay for health care is devoted to pharmaceuticals alone. This is an astonishing statistic when compared to the roughly 15% average in most of the developed world.

Its not just pills that are popping at premium prices. Doctors are also overprescribing new specialized treatments and tests. As yet another symptom of the corruption endemic in China, many sick people find that the only way to get proper care in a hospital is to offer so-called red-envelope bribes over and above their already exorbitant fees. Most heinously, according to China's own State Council Development Research Centre, some unscrupulous doctors have even "made patients more sick so they would buy more treatment." This poignant passage from the *Washington Post* aptly illustrates the cold and ruthless economic calculus that now serves as the centerpiece of China's shattered health-care system:

> On the day she arrived at the Number Three People's Hospital to seek treatment for HIV, Cai had no symptoms. But she did have a little bit of money, and that gets quick attention in the modern-day Chinese health-care system: The doctors pressured her to check in and begin a regimen of expensive intravenous drugs, warning that the alternative was a swift death.... When she asked for the free anti-AIDS drugs the central government had begun providing to the poor, the doctors rebuffed her...until she agreed to pay for costly tests. And when she ran through her money and all she could borrow—her 45-day hospital stay exceeding $1,400, nearly triple her annual income—the doctors cast her out. "The director told me to go away and wait until I had some money."

Given that the health-care system is in shambles, it is hardly surprising that infant mortality is again on the rise. The immunization rates for diseases such as TB, diphtheria, tetanus, and polio are steadily falling from levels that were close to 100% during the 1980s; and TB is again surging. Add a rapidly expanding HIV/AIDS crisis and the specter of exotic diseases such as bird flu and SARS, and you have all the ingredients of a health-care meltdown. As Richard McGregor of the *Financial Times* has put it: "The health system has become a kind of perfect storm for China's transition from a state to a market economy."

China's Ticking HIV/AIDS Time Bomb

They line the dusty roads outside the tiny villages of China's Henan Province, several hours' drive from Beijing—mounds of dirt funneled into crudely shaped cones, like a phalanx of earthen bamboo hats. To the uninitiated, they look like a clever new way of turning over fields—an agricultural innovation, perhaps, meant to increase crop yields. But the locals know the truth. Buried under the pyramids, which now number in the thousands, are their mothers and fathers, brothers, sisters, and cousins, all victims of AIDS. Like silent sentries, the dirt graves are a testament to China's worst-kept secret.

—Time

"To the government, we [AIDS victims] are like bubbles. They know if they turn away and ignore us, we will soon pop and be gone." But ignoring such people has become an increasingly difficult task as poor farmers, emboldened by desperation, are beginning to protest and speak out.

—New York Times

At present, it is India, not China, vying most ignominiously for the world reputation of worst future HIV crisis. Already, more than five million people have become infected in India. Because of a thriving heterosexual prostitution trade, strong cultural taboos against basic sex education, and widespread ignorance about prevention such as condom use, India's epidemic is projected to grow even more serious over time.

That said, many experts also believe that China's AIDS epidemic will eventually rival that of India's and dwarf that of all other countries. The reason may be found in one of the most tragic and shameful tales in the annals of economic history—that of China's "bloodheads."

The tale of the bloodheads begins in China's heartland in the early 1990s, in some of the most desperately poor rural provinces in the country—Anhui, Hebei, Hubei, Shandong, Shanxi, Shaanxi, and worst of all, Henan. Together, these seven provinces are home to more than 400 million people, and per-capita annual income hovers well below $500.

As part of China's economic reforms, bureaucrats hatched a plan to address rural poverty by capitalizing on high demand and high prices in both the domestic and international markets for blood and blood plasma. Initially, the government's efforts focused on simply collecting just blood, but they quickly realized that frequent donations dramatically increase the risk of anemia. To maximize profits— and to best boost peasant incomes—they discovered the best business model involved extracting the plasma from the peasants' blood and then re-injecting the red and white blood cells and corpuscle material back into the peasants. This prevented anemia, allowing peasants to contribute plasma much more frequently—as often as four to six days in a row with a few days rest in between.

The problem with the plan was the way doctors and nurses returned the peasants' blood after the plasma extraction. In Western hospital clinics, the plasma extraction can be done on an individual basis in a single pass. In China, however, it was a two-stage process in which blood was first drawn and the plasma separated. In the deadly second stage, doctors would *combine* the plasma-less blood into a *common pool* based on blood type. They would then draw from this common pool to re-inject blood into their donors. No more efficient way of spreading HIV, Hepatitis C, and other viruses has ever been created!

Now here is the even greater tragedy: When the Chinese bureaucracy figured out it was mass-producing HIV/AIDS victims as part of a poverty program, it stopped. However, the vacuum was filled by a cadre of entrepreneurs who had become, like the leaches of nineteenth-century medicine, part of the whole plasma business. These were the infamous bloodheads. As the Chinese bureaucracy rapidly retreated from its program, the bloodheads stepped in—and stepped up—the production of plasma and further accelerated the spread of the virus. This went on for years after the Chinese government outlawed the practice.

The net result of the bloodhead scandal has been to kill millions of Chinese and leave tens of thousands of children as orphans. It has also created a whole new class of disease spreaders. Combined with rapidly rising levels of intravenous drug use, the re-establishment of China's once flourishing flesh trade, and a 1960s-style "sexual revolution" in China's biggest cities—all of which constitute high-risk HIV/AIDS behaviors—the bloodheads have effectively set the stage for the worst AIDS crisis in the world.

According to the United Nations, China will have more HIV/AIDS victims than any other nation save perhaps India—as many as 10 to 15 million by 2010. This HIV/AIDS crisis will put a tremendous strain on a health-care system that as we have seen is already in tatters.

This compelling passage from the *Washington Post* illustrates the rage of China's mass of AIDS victims and how the boot-to-the-neck response of China's totalitarian government has only served to further inflame the Chinese countryside:

Xiong Jinglun was lying in bed on the night of the raid, resting his frail, AIDS-weakened body when the shouting outside jarred him awake. The 51-year-old farmer struggled to his feet and shuffled out of his shack to investigate, but someone had cut off the electricity in the village, and it was difficult to see in the pitch dark. Suddenly, several men wearing riot gear and military fatigues surrounded him, struck his head with a nightstick and knocked him to the ground. Xiong begged them to stop hitting him, crying out that he was an old man, that he had AIDS. But he heard one of the assailants shout: "Beat them! Beat them even if they have AIDS!" A few days earlier, residents of this AIDS-stricken Chinese village had staged a protest demanding better medical care, rolling two government vehicles into a ditch to vent their frustration. Now, local authorities here in central Henan Province, about 425 miles northwest of Shanghai, were answering their appeal for help. But instead of doctors, they sent the police. More than 500 officers, local officials, and hired thugs stormed the muddy hamlet of 600 residents on the night of June 21, shouting threats, smashing windows and randomly pummeling people who got in their way, witnesses said. Police jailed 18 villagers and injured more than a dozen others, including an eight-year-old boy who tried to defend his sick mother.

Muslim Separatists or "Terrorists"?

As Muslim ethnic minorities chafe under Chinese rule, a simmering revolt and seething ethnic conflict have turned much of western China into a heavily armed garrison ready to crush sporadic, spontaneous, and seemingly futile acts of rebellion.

—*New York Times*

The Chinese military in Xinjiang will always keep up the intensity of its crackdown on ethnic separatist forces and deal them devastating blows without showing any mercy.

—Xinjiang Party Secretary Wang Lequan

Almost 95% of China's population is classified as "ethnic Chinese" or "Han." However, not all of China's many wars from within are pitting Han "brother against brother." Ground zero for China's growing ethnic rebellions against the ruling Han class is the northwest province of Xinjiang.

Xinjiang is China's largest province geographically but, with its extremes of heat and cold, and its desert climate, Xinjiang is also one of its most sparsely populated. From an agricultural point of view, much of Xinjiang is a virtual dustbowl. However, beneath Xinjiang's dusty soil and mountainous steppes, 40% of China's coal reserves lie buried. Equally abundant and far more precious to the central government are oil and natural gas deposits that total the equivalent of about 30 billion tons of oil and represent one-fourth to one-third of China's total petroleum reserves.

In Xinjiang, the majority of the population consists of a Muslim Turkic people called the Uighurs. These Uighurs face some of the harshest and most repressive measures in the world under the jackboots of Chinese communism. Any independent religious activity can be equated to a "breach of state security"; activists are regularly arrested and tortured; and despite its sparse population, Xinjiang's ethnic groups suffer more executions for state-security crimes than any other province.

Tragically, repression in Xinjiang has only intensified in the wake of the 9/11 terrorist attacks on the United States. The Chinese government seized upon this American tragedy as a golden opportunity to cut a very clever deal with the United States. China would support the U.S. war on terrorism if the United States would agree that the separatist activities of the Uighurs represented not simply an indigenous rebellion against autocratic rule but rather a legitimate terrorist threat with ties to Al Qaeda and Osama Bin Laden. As part of its deal with America, China now defines a terrorist in Xinjiang as anyone who thinks "separatist thoughts," and Xinjiang's jails are crowded with such pseudo-terrorists.

Although China's iron-fisted repression in Xinjiang borders on the unbearable, what sticks most in the Uighur craw is the ongoing "Hanification" of Xinjiang. As a matter of policy, for decades the Chinese government has sought to pacify Xinjiang by importing large portions of its Han population from other, primarily poor areas—and even by despicably *exporting* young Uighur women of child-bearing age out of the region. Consider this chilling passage from Reuters:

> China's government is forcibly moving young women of the ethnic Uighur minority from their homes in Xinjiang to factories in eastern China, a Uighur activist told the U.S. Congress on Wednesday. Rebiya Kadeer, jailed for more than five years for championing the rights of the Muslim Uighurs before being sent into exile in the United States, called for U.S. help in stopping a program she said had already removed more than 240,000 people, mostly women, from Xinjiang. The women face harsh treatment with 12-hour workdays and often see wages withheld for months. ... Many suspect that the Chinese government policy is to get them to marry majority Han Chinese in China's cities while resettling Han in traditional Uighur lands.

Today, as a result of these policies, the Han population is rising at a rate twice as fast as that of the Uighur population. Instead of being pacified or tamed by the growing Han population, the Uighurs are just becoming more and more radicalized. There is a very bitter and dangerous irony in this ethnic strife reported in *The Economist:* Whereas the Uighurs historically have been "among the world's most liberal and pro-Western Muslims, fundamentalist Islam is gaining sway among young Uighur men." Today, "small-scale clashes break out nearly every day between Chinese and Uighurs in Xinjiang's western cities."

It is unlikely that a true guerrilla movement will emerge in Xinjiang to engage Chinese forces in an Algerian- or Vietnamese-style revolt. The populace is simply too small, and Chinese security forces are too big and powerful. However, in an age of "suitcase" nuclear bombs and biological terrorist weapons, China is exposed to terrorist threats at soft target points, such as the Three Gorges Dam, or any one of its teeming cities. Any such terrorist incidents could possibly help fuel conflicts in any one of a number of China's other "wars from within," making the severe repression of the Uighurs a risky strategy indeed.

In this chapter, we have seen both how and why the Communist Party is now facing ever-increasing opposition from China's downtrodden peasant farmers, its oppressed workers, its increasingly desperate senior citizens, and its ruthlessly suppressed ethnic minorities. Still other crises loom on the horizon, including rapidly rising income disparities and the kind of rampant inflation that sparked the Tiananmen Square uprising. In light of this growing opposition, it is hardly surprising that the Chinese government continues to escalate its efforts to spy upon, and ruthlessly crack down on, Chinese dissidents. The next chapter details in much greater detail just how "Big Brother" is alive, well, and ever-more Orwellian in what has morphed into the world's biggest prison.

9

Inside the World's Biggest Prison with Yahoo! the Stool Pigeon and Comrade Orwell

Congress shall make no law respecting an establishment of religion, or prohibiting the free exercise thereof; or abridging the freedom of speech, or of the press; or the right of the people peaceably to assemble, and to petition the Government for a redress of grievances.

—First Amendment to the U.S. Constitution

No one should ever confuse James Madison and Mao Zedong. Of these two "founding fathers," Mao laid the cornerstone for what has become the world's biggest police state and prison. In contrast, by introducing the Bill of Rights to the United States Constitution, James Madison helped guarantee every right and freedom now regularly and ruthlessly denied to the Chinese people.

Regrettably, many Americans take so many of their rights and freedoms for granted that it is almost impossible for U.S. citizens to fathom the level of repression the Chinese people must endure. Yet consider what it would be like to live in an America that operated under the same totalitarian rules as today's China. There would be

- No synagogue services on Friday nights or church on Sundays, and certainly no sermons from Billy Graham or "I Have a Dream" speeches from the likes of the late Martin Luther King Jr.

- No secret ballot voting for U.S. presidents on the first Tuesdays of November every four years—or openly complaining about the outcome on Wednesdays.

- No Fox News on the right, no *New York Times* on the left, and no toppling of any presidents by Woodward and Bernstein and the *Washington Post.*

- No hardball with Chris Mathews, softball with Tim Russert, or political satire from Jay Leno, David Letterman, or Jon Stewart.

- No consumer advocates like Ralph Nader to make our cars safer or "inconvenient truths" from environmentalists like Al Gore.

- No Erin Brockovich to crack down on corporate polluters, no Julia Roberts to play her in the movie, and no Mike Wallace and *60 Minutes* to crack down on everybody.

- And certainly no Betty Friedan or a women's movement.

Instead, in a Chinese version of today's America, each of these American politicians, personalities, pundits, and public advocates would long ago have rotted away in "reeducation through labor" prison camps, been beaten into submission, taken a bullet to the back of the head, or simply disappeared. This chapter explains exactly why this is so and what it is really like to live behind China's bamboo curtain. It is a chapter that should open the eyes of anyone who still harbors any democratic illusions about life in today's totally totalitarian China. It is also a chapter that illustrates in graphic detail what the ultimate political stakes might be if America and the rest of the world were ultimately to lose *The Coming China Wars.*

Let a Thousand Censors Snip

News publication has an important role in ideological education, and our country's security depends on strict control of news production.

—Chinese General Administration of Press and Publication

Chinese thought control begins with the near absence of a free press. Instead, for most Chinese citizens, all news flows from the official voice of the Communist Party and the world's biggest propaganda mill—the Xinhua news agency.

Each of Xinhua's almost 10,000 reporters undergo extensive political indoctrination from the government's aptly named Central Propaganda Department. As a group, these quasi-journalists are tasked with the job of producing "all the news that fits the party line" for more than 9,000 magazines, 2,000 newspapers, 300 radio stations, and 350 TV stations.

Even as Xinhua churns out its steady stream of propaganda, other competing tentacles of the Communist Party are employed in the most massive censorship operation the world has ever seen. In this Orwellian world, newspapers are routinely prohibited from reporting on a wide range of subjects, particularly government corruption. Coverage of public protests and events, such as environmental disasters, is likewise tightly restricted.

This is not to say that the zealotry of Chinese censorship doesn't occasionally border on the darkly comic. For example, foreigners living in Beijing frequently find that when their subscriptions to magazines such as *Time* and *Newsweek* arrive, the pages resemble the remains of a child's paper doll project. Offending sentences, whole articles, photos, and even the Victoria's Secret ads are cut out by hand—along with whatever happened to be on the opposite side.

Besides low comedy, Chinese censorship can also offer high irony. Even as China regularly excoriates Japan for its "revisionist history" of the Rape of Nanjing, Chinese propagandists have effectively erased all the articles, pictures, and videos documenting the Tiananmen Square massacre from the collective Chinese memory bank. As Exhibit A, there is that stark image of a single young man standing before a column of oncoming tanks that is so burned into Western minds; this image is virtually unknown in modern Beijing.

Of course, Chinese censorship is hardly limited to the print media. The government regularly jams radio broadcasts from sources ranging from the Voice of America (VOA) and Radio Free Asia (RFA) to the BBC. In addition, the only place you can see TV stations like CNN are in tourist hotels.

Fear and Loathing on the Not So World Wide Web

The Great Firewall of China is built with American bricks.

— Professor Kim Wu, Columbia Law School

In addition to spreading its propaganda through official Chinese news sources and censoring all print, radio, and TV media, China has built—with the extensive help of American corporations—its vaunted "Great Firewall of China."

Like a virtual fine-toothed comb, China's Great Firewall censors prowl 24/7 to block, filter, monitor, and control all of China's Internet traffic. In fact, this spying capability exists largely because of the sophisticated Internet network equipment that America's Cisco Systems has sold to China—while generating billions of dollars in revenue for Cisco shareholders.

Cisco is hardly the only American company helping China keep the jackboot to the neck of its people. Skype, an eBay subsidiary, helps the Chinese government monitor and censor text messaging. Microsoft's minions regularly help cleanse the Chinese blogosphere. Meanwhile, Google brainiacs have built a special version of their powerful search engine to filter out terms as diverse as the *BBC, Free Tibet,* and that four-letter word in China—*democracy.*

When China's Great Firewall does find a prohibited word or phrase, it automatically blocks the user's search. It might also issue a warning to the web surfer about "offending or pornographic speech." It may even shut down the user's web access for a brief period—or permanently.

As misdirection, the Great Firewall may also reroute a search on a term such as *human rights* to a Xinhua news agency page on China's "harmonious culture." As a further tactical measure, China's cyber cops often employ sophisticated "worms" to prevent any cyber-dissidents from trying to scale the Great Firewall. These worms are virus-like programs that have been specifically designed to burrow into dissident computers and destroy any encryption software designed to evade censorship.

Comrade Orwell Meets Yahoo! the Stool Pigeon

Morally, you are pygmies.

—Congressman Tom Lantos to Yahoo! executives

In addition to China's techno-fixes for Internet surveillance, there is an extensive army of "Internet Orwells" to keep an eye out for dissident Net traffic. Astonishingly, these Comrade Orwells number some 30,000 Chinese workers who help monitor Internet blogs and chat rooms. They also collaborate with the police to track down the most egregious offenders. In fact, China leads the world in jailed Internet users.

One highly publicized case further illustrates the complicity of American corporations in Chinese repression. In this case, the Chinese journalist Shi Tao was sentenced to ten years for one click of his subversive mouse. What Shi did was to forward an email from the government to a pro-democracy group that ordered the country's media not to report on the fifteenth anniversary of the Tiananmen Square protests.

When China's Internet Orwells uncovered this email, they pressured Yahoo! to reveal Shi's identity. Threatened with loss of access to the world's fastest-growing market, Yahoo! caved quicker than you can say Vichy France.

For ratting out Shi, Yahoo! Chief Executive Jerry Yang was dragged before Congress, called a "moral pygmy," and forced to issue an apology to Shi's mother, who sat behind Yang at the hearing. In sharp contrast to Yang's public shaming, however, Cisco's Chief Executive John Chambers has received little public scrutiny for his company's role as chief architect of China's Great Firewall.

Business executives like Cisco's Chambers justify their actions with a "when in China, do as the Chinese do" defense. To do business in China, these executives insist, they must comply with local laws. But China's local laws often force executives to make moral and ethical choices that would be intolerable in the West.

The broader problem is that American business executives have little training in how to deal with ethics in a corrupt and totalitarian global business environment such as China—blame U.S. business schools for that. As a result, moral horizons tend to be short, and executives who find themselves in the heat of a battle don't know where to draw the line, which is what happened to Yahoo!

What's missing from the American corporate perspective is this bigger picture: The collaborative tools that U.S. corporations provide to spy on, and silence, the Chinese people are much more likely to help prop up a totalitarian regime than topple it.

Who Are the Major Targets of Chinese Repression?

By now, it should be clear that China runs the biggest propaganda mill in the world, engages in the most extensive censorship on the planet, and has the most sophisticated Internet control system U.S.

companies have ever helped devise. At this juncture, it is useful to circle back and look more closely at who the major targets of Chinese repression are.

Fear Is Mightier Than the Pen

Journalism has become the third most dangerous job in China after mining and the police.

—Reporters Without Borders

Some of the biggest targets of Chinese repression are home-grown Chinese journalists. Soft targets include any journalists who stray from the party line. Hard targets include investigative journalists who seek to report on anything from government corruption or a new environmental disaster to the latest beating of a human rights activist or jailing of a Sunday worshiper.

As Human Rights Watch has noted, foreign journalists seeking to break through the bamboo curtain are also "routinely harassed, detained and intimidated by Chinese government officials, security forces, and plainclothes thugs who appear to operate at official behest."

Because of the high risks of practicing freedom of the press, self-censorship has become one of the most important rules of journalistic self-preservation in today's China. Domestic journalists engage in self-censorship to avoid beatings, harassment, or jail. Foreign journalists will often engage in self-censorship to avoid being expelled from the country, rationalizing that half a story is better than none.

A *Strangled* Vox Populi

Although the Chinese constitution guarantees freedom of association and assembly, national regulations severely limit association and give the authorities absolute discretion to deny applications for public gatherings or demonstrations. In practice, only organizations that are approved by the authorities are permitted to exist, and any organization that is not registered is considered "illegal." In this manner, independent advocacy on labor, human rights, environmental, development, or political issues is effectively outlawed.

—U.S. Department of State

A second major target of China's jackboots is represented by any and all pro-democracy voices and political activists. Included in this target group are both mass protesters and individual petitioners.

On the pro-democracy front, all words such as *democracy, freedom,* and *liberty* are verboten. On the political activist front, those in the crosshairs include advocates for civil rights, human rights, women's rights, and workers' rights. Targets also include everyone from seniors seeking better pensions and health care to HIV-AIDS activists.

Public protesters are dealt with particularly harshly. So, too, are the millions of petitioners who stream into Beijing each year seeking relief from all manner of local and provincial corruption and abuse.

There is no small paradox in the harsh treatment petitioners receive. As noted by *Human Rights News,* "China's petitioning system has a long cultural and historical tradition dating back to the beginnings of the Chinese empire." However, in today's China, cracking down on petitioners has become a lucrative growth industry for Chinese thugs. As reported by RFA, the government regularly employs such thugs to terrorize petitioners, and they are paid "according to the number of petitioners captured and beaten."

Besides common thugs, there also exists "petitioner retrievers." They are "typically recruited and paid by local government officials who fear a loss of face before the eyes of the national government in Beijing. Their job is to attack and intimidate petitioners and force them to return to their home province. Beijing police, in turn, play their part: to quell the threat of rising discontent. They raze the shantytowns where petitioners live in Beijing, round up petitioners, and hand them over to the retrievers, turning a blind eye to the retaliatory violence."

Big Brother Is a Bully in the Pulpit

Citizens of the People's Republic of China enjoy freedom of religious belief.

—Article 36 of the Constitution

China has sentenced a key house church leader "to one year re-education through labor" for explaining the Gospel of Jesus Christ to a Communist Party official. Gu Changrong, 54, was detained March 14 by local police in Fushun city in China's Liaoning province while "sharing her Christian faith," with the secretary of the Communist Party of her village, who was identified as Yu Mingfu. Three Public Security Bureau officers took Gu away, and soon after, she received the one year forced labor sentence on charges of "using evil cult organizations to obstruct the exercising of state laws.

—Mt. Zion Report

Kneel before God and wind up in the slammer? That is the reality in today's China—even as government officials desperately try to convince the world otherwise.

While the Chinese Communist Party is officially atheist, it does recognize five religions: Buddhism, Taoism, Islam, Protestantism, and Catholicism. There is, however, a very big bump on China's cul de sac to religious freedom.

In particular, all churches, mosques, pagodas, and temples must first register with the Chinese government. The Chinese government then has the right to control the affairs of that institution; and such control is far-reaching. It includes who runs the church, what information can be distributed to worshipers, when services can be held, the size of gatherings, and almost all other aspects of an institution's operations.

Under such tight restrictions, many religious leaders choose not to register their institutions with the government. Many worshipers likewise prefer to attend unregistered "house churches" to avoid being watched by the government. This is particularly true for worshipers who are members of the Communist Party, because Party members are officially discouraged from practicing a religion.

As a result of China's "Big Brother in the pulpit" approach, thousands of "house churches" have sprung up in back rooms and basements across China; but attending a house church can be very dangerous. As noted by *USA Today*, the Chinese government annually rounds up thousands of unauthorized worshipers. These edited excerpts from the Christian Newswire offer just one small glimpse of how the Chinese Grinch annually steals Christmas—while regularly assaulting the house church network year round:

> **Jiangsu Province:** A house church in Chang Zhou City was attacked by police officials in December during a Christmas celebration. The church, led by Pastor Bu Ge Qiao, was in the midst of a Christmas service when police raided the gathering and detained four female members. During the apprehension, police assaulted one of the members until she became unconscious. She was later taken to the hospital. Her condition remains unknown.
>
> **Henan Province:** On December 16, less than two weeks before Christmas, Pastor Liang Qi Zhen was detained by PSB officials in Er Qi District. After disbursing Liang's congregation, police officials took him by force and transported him to an undisclosed location where he was tortured for several hours. Liang's ears and right hand were injured during the lengthy assault.

Using Tibetan Nuns and Monks as Target Practice

If the matter of Tibet's sovereignty is murky, the question about the PRC's treatment of Tibetans is all too clear. After invading Tibet in 1950, the Chinese communists killed over one million Tibetans, destroyed over 6,000 monasteries, and turned Tibet's northeastern province, Amdo, into a gulag housing up to ten million people. In addition, some 7.5 million Chinese have responded to Beijing's incentives to relocate to Tibet; they now outnumber the six million Tibetans. Through what has been termed Chinese apartheid, ethnic Tibetans now have a lower life expectancy, literacy rate, and per capita income than Chinese inhabitants of Tibet.

—The Heritage Foundation

Whether Tibet is rightfully the territory of China or not is a question that trails murkily back into a long and twisting history of dueling Chinese dynasties and Tibetan Dalai Lamas. In many ways, it is a moot question because China is unlikely to ever provide Tibet with any real autonomy—much less the independence that members of groups like Free Tibet insist upon.

What is not murky at all are the incredible abuses and repression that ordinary Tibetans are exposed to every day under Chinese occupation. There is also nothing murky about why Tibet is so highly coveted by the Chinese government.

Consider first that the Chinese word for Central Tibet is *Xizang*. It means "western treasure house." The treasure in question refers to the fact that Tibet is a repository for some of the world's largest deposits of boron, borax, chromite, iron, lithium, and uranium. In addition, Tibet has significant reserves of oil and natural gas, gold and silver, and copper and zinc and contains a treasure trove of lesser-known minerals ranging from arsenic, cesium, corundum, and graphite to magnesite, mica, sulphur, titanium, and vanadium.

In addition to its mineral wealth, Tibet—literally translated as "the heights"—has some of the biggest hydro-electric power potential in the world. The headwaters of China's two largest rivers—the Yellow and Yangtze—lie high in Tibet's northeastern and eastern provinces and account for four-fifths of China's water. Massive dams in Tibet are already helping to light up and power much of western China.

China's current reign of repression dates back to 1950 when China invaded Tibet. A 1951 treaty was supposed to guarantee Tibet's autonomy, but China failed to hold up its end of the bargain. The eventual result was a 1959 revolt, the slaughter of more than a million Tibetans, and the exile of Tibet's spiritual leader, the Dalai Lama, to India.

According to Human Rights Watch, "Chinese authorities view the exiled Dalai Lama as the linchpin of the effort to separate Tibet from China and view Tibetan Buddhist belief as supportive of his efforts. Thus, the government limits the number of monasteries and monks, vets all applicants for the monkhood, interferes with the selection of monastic leaders, prohibits performance of traditional rites, and conducts ongoing reeducation campaigns centered on opposition to the Dalai Lama."

Even today, Buddhists loyal to the Dalai Lama continue to be hunted like dogs in the mountains by Chinese troops. In Berlin Wall–style executions, nuns and monks are shot in cold blood while attempting to make their escape to Nepal or India. Just consider this recent passage from the *London Independent*:

> A few minutes of jerky video footage shot by a Romanian cameraman on a mountaineering trip brought the plight of Tibetans under Chinese rule into Western living rooms this month. For once, the world was able to watch the cruelty of occupation as it played out. In the video, a Chinese border guard calmly opens fire from a mountain ridge on a group of unarmed, defenseless Tibetans below, as they struggled

through the snow to escape from occupied Tibet. Two figures drop to the ground. Said one of the survivors, "we were walking in line. Before the shooting, we knew the soldiers were after us so we started to walk quickly. They warned us to stop, and then they started shooting. We were running. The bullets were landing near us. The nun who died was 100 metres ahead of me. I saw her fall down. I was lucky. A bullet tore my trousers, but it missed me."

Who's Afraid of the Falun Gong?

Just after sunrise, in virtually every park and town square in China, clusters of people glide in unison through a set of tranquil, ritualized movements known as qigong, *prosaically translated as "breathing exercises" but representing an alluring blend of spiritualism and physical exertion. There are few sights more common across China's vast breadth. But a buzz has developed around one particular breathing master Li Hongzhi whose exercises, his followers believe, can not only cure cancer and turn white hair black again, but also provide moral and spiritual guidance. Millions of Chinese are his Falun Gong adherents—so many that the government is visibly concerned.*

—*Time*, May 1999

China today banned the Research Society of Falun Dafa and the Falun Gong organization under its control after deeming them to be illegal. In its decision on this matter issued today, the Ministry of Civil Affairs said that according to investigations, the Research Society of Falun Dafa had not been registered according to law and had been engaged in illegal activities, advocating superstition and spreading fallacies, hoodwinking people, inciting and creating disturbances, and jeopardizing social stability.

—Communist Party Directive, July 1999

Before the Communist Party banned the Falun Gong, it boasted well over 70 million adherents. Today, no one knows how many adherents remain. In one of the most massive and merciless human rights violations in history, virtually all of China's Falun Gong have been driven underground, put into prison, forced to publicly renounce their beliefs, or been executed.

Just what is Falun Gong? Why did the Chinese government ban it? Is it really the dangerous cult the Chinese government would have us believe?

Falun Gong is a modern-day amalgam of three elements of ancient Chinese philosophical and religious traditions. Two of these elements—Chinese Buddhism and Taoism—provide Falun Gong with its moral philosophy. The third element—Qigong—is similar in many ways to Indian yoga. Qigong provides Falun Gong with its set of physical movements, postures, and breathing exercises designed to promote health, improve concentration, and serve as meditation.

Falun Gong was introduced into China in 1992 by a charismatic former musician and grain clerk named Li Hongzhi. Through his videotapes, books, and lectures, Li would go on to develop a following of more than 70 million in seven short years.

While the Chinese government has used the argument that Falun Gong is a cult, most of its allegedly "cult-like" qualities are not unlike characteristics that can be found in religions and movements freely practiced throughout the rest of the world.

For example, like the Christian Science Church, Falun Gong practitioners believe in the power of the mind and spirit in healing. In fact, much of the popularity of the Falun Gong in the 1990s has been attributed to the loss of universal health care as China turned into a capitalist economy.

Like the proponents of transcendental meditation, Falun Gong practitioners speak (perhaps metaphorically) of being able to fly, levitate, become invisible, or walk through walls—all by harnessing the life force of the body.

These metaphysical (and phantasmagorical) elements aside, most of what Falun Gong is about is a mind-body experience not unlike that of Buddhism or Christianity designed to promote health, strength, moral character, and spirituality. If that is so, why has the Chinese police state all but eradicated Falun Gong? The answer may be found in a fundamental political error committed by Li Hongzhi in peacefully challenging the authority of the state in 1999. The precipitating event is aptly described in *Time* magazine:

> To register their displeasure over government treatment of the group, 10,000 of Li's followers suddenly assembled on April 25 on the sidewalks around Zhongnanhai, the high-security complex that houses China's top leaders, and sat in meditative postures along a two kilometer stretch. The demonstration was peaceful, entirely unexpected, and the largest organized show of opposition since the Tiananmen democracy movement in 1989. It ended quietly, with the protesters even picking up their own litter, but only after 12 hours, an audience within Zhongnanhai with Premier Zhu Rongji and his aides, and a government promise that the group's grievances would be addressed within three days.

What the Falun Gong got from this event was not a fulfillment of the government's promise to address its grievances within three days. Instead, within three months, the government—terrified by the largest mass demonstration it had seen since 1989 in Tiananmen Square—launched a full-scale assault on every Falun Gong practitioner in China.

China's assault on the Falun Gong was every bit as rabid as the worst excesses of the Cultural Revolution. It relied on both the army and police to conduct mass arrests. Tens of thousands of Falun Gong practitioners were put into prisons, reeducation through labor (RTL) camps, or psychiatric hospitals. In addition, employers were ordered to fire any Falun Gong who refused to renounce his or her beliefs, and schools were used to indoctrinate children against the Falun Gong movement.

This first-person account from a prisoner in a Chinese labor camp provides stark testimony to the horrors that have rained down upon the Falun Gong in China:

> I was detained in Beijing's Female Forced Labor Camp because I believe in and practice Falun Gong. I was illegally arrested at my home, and during my detention, I was repeatedly subjected to inhuman torture. I was often deprived of food. For long periods of time, I was not allowed to sleep or to use the bathroom. The guards often ordered the criminal inmates to beat me up. In order to muffle my cries, the guards stuffed dirty underwear, stained with menstrual blood from other females, into my mouth. I was beaten until my body was completely covered with bruises.
>
> There was a practitioner who was sent here from the detention center. Her head had been twisted about 150 degrees, and almost faced her back. In the detention center, she had received excruciating torture because she refused to renounce Falun Gong. The guards then twisted her lower back, handcuffed her hands and feet together while she was in that twisted position, and kept her like that for over ten days. A person in her 40s had, through torture, been made to look like someone in her 70s, simply because she held fast to her belief in Truthfulness-Compassion-Forbearance.

Nothing to Fear but Fear Itself—And That's (Usually) Enough

My guiding principle is this: Guilt is never to be doubted.

—Franz Kafka

While tens of millions of brave souls challenge China's Orwellian state each year, they represent but a medium-size drop of dissidence in a 1.4 billion population bucket. In fact, like those cowed journalists who succumb to self-censorship, the overwhelming majority of Chinese citizens assiduously toe the Party line.

Some Chinese citizens embrace civil obedience simply because the economic times have been good to them. However, the far bigger element in China's docility equation is the raw stench of a gut-wrenching, sweat-stained fear. This fear begins with the total absence of nearly every freedom guaranteed in the U.S. Bill of Rights and ends in a system of injustice that would make Franz Kafka's skin crawl. In China's "Kafka on steroids" legal system, there are

- **No search warrants, protections against false arrest, or bail.** Chinese authorities can knock down any doors to collect evidence and have extremely broad powers of arrest. Political and religious targets may be charged with anything ranging from revealing state secrets and subversion to trumped-up charges of common crimes such as blackmail or extortion. Most defendants taken into custody are denied bail, and many are put into "incommunicado detention," with no notification to their family.

- **No adequate legal representation.** Defense lawyers are subject to all manner of abuse and intimidation. They may be unlawfully detained, beaten, and/or disbarred. Under a catchall clause in the Chinese legal system, defense lawyers may also be arrested and charged if their client commits perjury, offers "false testimony," or fabricates evidence; and prosecutors have a very broad definition of just what constitutes these offenses.

- **No presumed innocence.** Like the officer in Franz Kafka's book *In the Penal Colony*, "Guilt is never to be doubted." In fact, as a bit of gallows humor, the term *xian pan hou shen* is used by citizens to describe China's system of "verdict first, trial second." Guilt is determined *before* the defendant's trial by a prosecution committee. Perhaps not surprisingly, conviction rates hover above 99%. Appeals of guilty verdicts are successful less than half of 1% of the time.

- **No trial by jury, witnesses, or right to remain silent.** During trials, defendants do not have the right to confront their accusers, and less than 5% of trials involve witnesses.

There is no right to remain silent, no protection against double jeopardy, and very few rules of evidence to limit what can be introduced by the state to convict a defendant.

- **No protections against cruel and unusual punishment.** Once someone is in a Chinese slammer, prison guards will continue to exert strong pressure if the person fails to acknowledge guilt. This is consistent with China's legal dictum of "lenience for those who confess, severity for those who resist."

  In some cases, prison guard pressures are limited to denying the inmate the right to buy food from the outside, to make any phone calls, or be visited. In other cases, as documented by the United Nations, inmates are subjected to all manners of torture and abuse—from beatings, cigarette burns, and submersion in water or sewage to shackles, sexual abuse, solitary confinement, and being tied up in grossly twisted positions for extended periods.

- **No conviction necessary for incarceration.** You don't have to be convicted to wind up incarcerated. "House arrest" is one common control and punishment measure that is often applied to political dissidents, petitioners, or religious practitioners—as well as their families.

  In a gambit that would make Big Nurse (of *One Flew Over the Cuckoo's Nest* infamy) proud, the Chinese government also frequently uses its psychiatric hospitals to "reeducate" or brainwash dissidents. In these institutions, prisoner patients are given all manner of mind-altering medicines against their will and forcibly subjected to electric shock "therapy." According to the U.S. State Department, prisoners are also "strapped to beds or other devices for days at a time, beaten, and denied food and use of toilet facilities."

- **No repressive stone left unturned.** The worst of China's prisons that claim not to be prisons are China's dreaded Reeducation Through Labor (RTL) camps. Individuals can be squirreled away for up to four years in an RTL camp, and they need not be formally charged or brought before a judge.

China's RTL camps are part of a broader latticework of Soviet-style gulags known as *laogai* that house as many as 20 million Chinese prisoners of conscience. This ultra-cheap prison labor helps China's mercantilist manufacturing machine do everything from farming, loading construction rock, and mining coal to producing finished goods such as toys and textiles.

Time is very hard in the laogai. Prisoners work nine to ten hours a day with only one day off every two weeks. They may work as many as 12 hours a day if timetables are not being met.

- **No protections against "capitalist" punishment.** China executes more prisoners than any other country in the world. As recently as 2001, a prisoner would be shot in the back of the head, and his family would be billed for the cost of the bullet. Often, these executions were carried out in public venues such as sports stadiums to cheering mobs and broadcast on TV.

Today, with greater concern about its world image, China prefers more private executions using lethal injections. The use of lethal injections is not for humane considerations. Rather, one major reason for the switch from bullets is China's headlong capitalist plunge into the organ-trafficking business.

As noted by Amnesty International, unlike a bullet, a lethal injection leaves the whole body intact, and organs, such as hearts, lungs, kidneys, and corneas, can "be extracted in a speedier and more effective way than if the prisoner is shot." According to China's own vice minister of health, the majority of organs used in transplants in China are extracted from executed prisoners.

As part of its highly efficient supply chain for its organ-trafficking business, China's capital punishment entrepreneurs have even invested in a large fleet of "death mobiles." These RV-size, rolling chambers of doom come equipped with police lights on the top and a complete medically staffed lethal injection facility. They are large enough to hold a prisoner, several guards, a judge, and an executioner. They typically park right outside a court to await the verdict and sentencing, and they can swiftly deliver fresh corpses or organs to transplant hospitals.

From China's Police State Blotter

This chapter ends with a short series of cases collected and edited from organizations such as Human Rights Watch, Human Rights in China, and Amnesty International. Some are particularly graphic, so please move on to the next chapter if you find them too unsettling. These cases do, however, help shed additional light on the level of Chinese repression—and the high stakes involved in fighting and winning *The Coming China Wars*:

- Beijing-based rights defense lawyer Li Heping was abducted by a group of unidentified masked men and then beaten and tortured with electric rods in a basement outside Beijing. The following day he was dumped in the woods outside the city and told to leave Beijing with his family. When Li returned home, he discovered that his license to practice law and other personal belongings were missing. His computer had also been completely erased.

- Yang Chunlin, a land rights activist, had his arms and legs stretched and chained to four corners of an iron bed in prison. According to a released inmate who served time with Yang, he was chained for days in the same position, and then was forced to clean up the excrement of other prisoners subjected to the same torture.

- Hunan petitioner Liu Ping was forcibly admitted to a psychiatric hospital. This resulted from her petitions to Beijing on the local government's failure to provide compensation after the factory where she worked went bankrupt.

- Hangzhou-based writer Lu Gengsong was taken into custody on charges of "incitement to subvert state power" and "illegally possessing state secrets." According to Lu's daughter, police officers from Hangzhou's Xihu District Cuiyuan Dispatch Station called Lu in for a talk, and he never came home. Subsequently, several state security police searched Lu's home and took his computer hard drive. Police prevented Lu's wife from going to Beijing to petition on Lu's behalf, and threatened that if she proceeded, she would be dismissed from her job and her daughter's schooling would be affected.

- Blind legal activist Chen Guangcheng was formally arrested after nine months of informal house arrest during which local officials physically abused Chen several times. Officials threatened attorneys and law professors who rallied to defend Chen. Local authorities proceeded to obstruct attempts by lawyers to gather evidence in Chen's defense; and the night before Chen's trial, Chen's lawyers were detained on spurious charges so that they could not represent him. Chen's court-appointed attorneys effectively conceded the case against him, and he was sentenced to four years in prison.

- Guards at the notorious Masanjia Labor Camp stripped 18 women naked and threw them into cells of violent male criminals where they were gang-raped.

10

Red Army Rising—The Coming China Hot Wars

The first rule of unrestricted warfare is that there are no rules, with nothing forbidden.

—Chinese air force Colonels Qiao Ling and Wang Xiangsui

We must persist in taking the development path of peaceful rise … and make a contribution to the lofty cause of peace and development for all humanity.

—Communist Party General Secretary Hu Jintao

Will China give us "unrestricted warfare" as its Young Turk military commanders have threatened or a "peaceful rise" as China's civilian leaders promise? Perhaps no question is bigger than this one in the twenty-first century because any "hot war" with China runs the very real risk of quickly escalating into a literally earth-shattering nuclear exchange. Compelling evidence against China's claim of a peaceful rise may be found in the following observations.

China is now engaged in a massive military buildup, with its military budget growing at almost twice the rate as China's own white-hot economy. Even more ominously, the Chinese military has dramatically shifted its strategic perspective. In the past, China focused primarily on the regional, and largely passive, defense of its territory. Today, China is beginning to project its military power globally while it focuses on the growing need to ensure access to international markets, global oil reserves, and other natural resources.

China's top strategic thinkers are also redefining the modern battlefield as well as the very concept of war itself. Just consider these chilling observations from the "asymmetrical warfare" playbook of air force Colonels Qiao Ling and Wang Xiangsui:

> If the attacking side secretly musters large amounts of capital without the enemy nation being aware of this at all and launches a sneak attack against its financial markets, then after causing a financial crisis, buries a computer virus and hacker detachment in the opponent's computer system in advance, while at the same time carrying out a network attack against the enemy so that the civilian electricity network, traffic-dispatching network, financial transactions network, telephone communications network, and mass-media network are completely paralyzed, this will cause the enemy nation to fall into social panic, street riots, and a political crisis.

This chapter takes a tough hard look at China's rapid military buildup together with its radical strategic shift toward unrestricted and asymmetrical warfare. Importantly, this chapter will also look at eight possible triggers for an actual hot war involving China's armed forces and potential combatants around the world.

Lest anyone believe that this hot war threat is fanciful, it is useful to remember this critical slice of modern Chinese history: Since the birth of communist China in 1949, China has fought border wars with both India and Vietnam. It has gone to the nuclear brink with Russia and fought proxy wars against the United States in both Taiwan and Vietnam. And one should never forget that the "Korean" War was primarily a very bloody, up-close, and personal battle between Chinese and American troops.

Turning Wal-Mart Plowshares into Chinese Swords

China has the greatest potential to compete militarily with the United States and field disruptive military technologies that could over time offset traditional U.S. military advantages.

—U.S. Department of Defense

The godfather of Communism—Vladimir Lenin—once famously remarked that a capitalist will sell you the rope to hang him with. As an ironic variation on that theme, America is now financing China's massive military buildup by running equally massive trade deficits with China.

The primary "financiers" of China's military buildup are American consumers who continue to load up on all things made in China. The resultant billions of "Wal-Mart dollars" sent off to China are now being used to radically modernize the People's Liberation Army, buy lethal nuclear submarines and aircraft carriers for the Chinese navy, and finance the purchase of sophisticated Russian aircraft for the Chinese air force.

Consider the People's Liberation Army. It features the largest ground force in the world—about 1.6 million personnel. In times of crisis, China can mobilize an additional 1.5 million reservists as well as the 1.1 million personnel now serving in the People's Armed Police. This all adds up to a very significant troop strength advantage over the United States.

This U.S.-China troop imbalance has very real strategic implications. For example, the failure of the American military to quickly "win the peace" after invading Iraq was the direct result of its inability to provide adequate troop strength in the days and months following the crushing military defeat of Saddam Hussein's forces. Whereas

U.S. military commanders would have preferred as many as half a million troops to keep the peace and rebuild Iraq's infrastructure, these commanders had to settle for less than 200,000 troops to police a country of almost 30 million citizens. The results of America's inadequate troop strength have been a disastrous insurgency, an exceedingly bloody vulnerability to foreign provocateurs such as Al Qaeda, and the steady and disturbing drift towards an Iraqi civil war. Chinese military commanders will never face any such manpower problem as they prepare to militarily engage worldwide.

As for the Chinese navy, it has a fleet of almost 100 ships and more than 50 submarines. This includes a new generation of high-tech nuclear subs that have significantly extended China's ballistic missile range from 1,000 miles to 5,000 miles. Running silent and deep, China's latest subs can now "nuke" American cities—from Los Angeles and San Francisco to Chicago and Detroit. China's new subs are also heavily armed with Russian-built cruise missiles specifically designed to attack and sink U.S. aircraft carriers—from the Taiwan Strait and Strait of Malacca to the Strait of Hormuz.

China's navy has also invested heavily in Russian-made cruise missile-equipped destroyers. These ships have already bullied Japanese civilian ships in the East China Sea and Sea of Japan in a dispute over oil and represent an important intimidating force in the region. At the same time, China is developing a significant "deepwater navy" capability replete with aircraft carriers to challenge the only other deepwater navy on the planet, that of the United States. This deepwater navy will ultimately be capable of projecting power around the world—from the coasts of Venezuela and Cuba to the Horn of Africa and beyond.

Complementing these army and navy forces is an increasingly potent Chinese air force. It now boasts more than 2,000 combat aircraft, including a growing number of highly sophisticated Russian jet fighters that strongly rival the performance of their American counterparts. At the same time, China is rapidly modernizing its ballistic missile program. Old technology, difficult-to-handle, liquid-propelled missiles are quickly giving way to more sophisticated solid fuel rockets which are much more mobile and easier to conceal.

Finally, as the centerpiece of its electronic warfare capabilities, China is rapidly developing an extensive capability to intercept and jam military intelligence and communications. To this end, and as I discuss in more detail in the next chapter, China has put into orbit several spacecrafts to support its military missions and is rapidly developing a sophisticated anti-satellite strike capability to render U.S. military systems "deaf, dumb, and blind" in time of war.

Clearly, the picture now emerging from China is not one of a country intent on a peaceful rise, but rather a budding military power clearly on the strategic prowl. At this point, it is useful to ask: Just what is motivating China's military buildup?

China's History of Violence

The modern Chinese state was born in war, barely survived its infancy because of the Korean War, engaged in a bitter contest with its erstwhile Soviet partner, waged a proxy war with the United States in Vietnam, engaged in border clashes with India and Vietnam, and then moved into an era of low intensity struggle with Taiwan and its American protector. The enduring climate of tensions and unresolved disputes has shaped the country's industrial plans and guided its diplomacy.

—John Wilson, *Imagined Enemies*

To understand what is motivating China's military buildup, it is critical to view the world from the Chinese military bridge. From that perspective, Chinese military officers fear attack, particularly a nuclear attack, from at least four countries: Japan, India, Russia, and the United States. This is not a completely irrational fear.

Consider Japan. It currently does not have nuclear weapons. However, Japan does have one of the largest and most sophisticated electricity-generating nuclear power plant capabilities in the world. Given its expertise, Japan can quickly develop a powerful arsenal of advanced nuclear weapons should it decide to remilitarize.

Thus far, Japan has resisted any urge to join the nuclear club. However, Chinese political and military leaders are well aware that there are growing pressures on Japan to rearm. Part of this pressure is coming from within Japan as frictions between China and Japan continue to grow over issues ranging from trade and energy to the environmental fallout from China that quite literally rains down on Japan. However, part of this pressure is also coming from the United States, which sees Japan as an important counterweight to the emergence of China as a regional power.

The United States is exerting similar political pressure on India, which the United States likewise views as a possible strategic counterweight to the nonpeaceful rise of China. In fact, tensions and mistrust between China and India have remained high ever since China started the Sino-India War of 1962 with a surprise attack. This war, which resulted in a humiliating Indian defeat, was triggered by a border dispute that continues to simmer to this day. India's humiliation has, in turn, triggered a dramatic increase in the military capabilities of India, including its development of nuclear weapons.

As for Russia, China shares a very long border with the Russian Bear—as well as a very long history of conflict. While today Russia is a major supplier of energy and weapons to China, in the yesterdays of this relationship, there have been numerous fights, including Soviet support for India during the Sino-Indian War and a rush to the nuclear brink in 1969 during an intense border skirmish. As for what tomorrow will bring in Sino-Russian relations, it is anyone's guess. But neither country trusts the other, and both have nuclear weapons pointed at each other.

Regarding China's perception of the possibilities of war with the United States, this is hardly an irrational fear either. The most likely trigger for such a confrontation, at least in the short run, would be a battle for Taiwan.

Fear and Loathing in the Taiwan Strait

A-bombs can be used as you would use a bullet.

—President Dwight D. Eisenhower

If the Americans draw their missiles and position-guided ammunition on to the target zone on China's territory, I think we will have to respond with nuclear weapons.

—General Zhu Chenghu, Chinese Defence University

When Mao Zedong and his Communist Party took over China in 1949, the deposed president, Chiang Kai-shek, fled to Taiwan with almost one million of his troops and immediately began planning for a counterrevolution. In 1953, as part of his plans to retake China, Chiang massed almost 75,000 troops on two islands just 8 miles off the coast of mainland China—Matsu and Quemoy. Mao's China quickly responded with a bombardment of Quemoy and the battle for Taiwan was on.

It is critical to note that at this historical juncture President Dwight Eisenhower was under great pressure from hardliners to respond with a nuclear strike against China. While Eisenhower resisted this pressure, China took very serious note of America's potential nuclear threat. This was particularly true in light of Eisenhower's regrettable claim that "A-bombs can be used as you would use a bullet," and the fact that the United States sent Quemoy and Matsu eight-inch howitzers capable of firing nuclear shells.

The first battle over Taiwan would drag on for years, and it would involve extensive fighting between Chinese and Taiwanese forces. Two pivotal events would occur when the United States sent in a U.S. naval force and provided Taiwan with air-to-air missiles that very effectively knocked China's Russian-made MIGs out of the sky. In October 1958, surprised by the ferocity of the American response, the Chinese minister of national defense negotiated a peaceful settlement that would effectively end hot war hostilities for more than 20 years.

The next confrontation over Taiwan would be triggered in 1995 by, of all things, a visit by the president of Taiwan to a Cornell University reunion. During the trip, Taiwan's president repeatedly referred to the "Republic of China on Taiwan," and this was interpreted in Beijing as a challenge to the so-called One China Policy upon which peace had implicitly rested. The essence of this One China Policy is that Taiwan would tacitly agree that it was part of China, but mainland China would leave Taiwan alone in a state of undeclared independence.

Provoked by the Cornell visit, the Chinese military began a set of missile tests in the vicinity of Taiwan; the Chinese air force moved a number of aircraft to the coast; and Beijing redeployed forces to coastal areas facing Taiwan amid rumors of preparations for a missile attack on Taiwan. Tensions were then further heightened by the appearance of the American naval fleet in the area.

From these confrontations with the United States in the Taiwan Strait, China has learned three important lessons now shaping its military strategy and modernization program. First, China's historic reliance on ground troops is insufficient in a world of U.S. air superiority. Second, the nuclear threat from the United States, coupled with China's wish to become more independent from what was then the Soviet Union, led China to develop its own nuclear weapons arsenal. Third, China was forced to understand in a much more visceral way the importance of naval superiority—and thus began its quest for a deepwater navy.

Today, conventional troops and heavy armaments continue to play an important role in the Taiwan Strait—as close to a half million Chinese troops stand ready to invade Taiwan. In addition, each year China adds another hundred or so low-range ballistic missiles to its arsenal aimed at Taiwan. This is an arsenal that already totals close to a thousand missiles. It is for this reason that Taiwan continues to rank number one as the most likely hot war trigger between China and the United States. However, Taiwan is hardly the only trigger that the world must be concerned about in the now unfolding story of *The Coming China Hot Wars.*

A Panoply of Hot War Triggers

Even though military officers as a rule are more conscious of the human cost of war than civilian politicians, eventually the generals may want to use the destroyers, submarines, and jet fighters that these big budgets have bought. War could be the by-product of the military buildup.

—Susan Shirk, *China: Fragile Superpower*

U.S. Defense Department analysts now carefully monitoring China's massive military buildup rightfully fear this: The more capable the Chinese military becomes and the more global the reach of its troops, missiles, satellite systems, and deepwater navy, the more likely China will engage militarily with the United States or other nations such as Russia, Taiwan, Vietnam, or Japan.

Trigger 1: Iran's Nuclear Follies

The United States and key countries in Europe such as Germany, France, and Great Britain have put intense pressure on Iran to back off from its efforts to develop its nuclear capabilities. At the same time, China has been busy peddling both conventional weapons and highly sophisticated nuclear technology to this rogue fundamentalist regime in exchange for access to Iranian oil and natural gas reserves. If Iran resumes its quest for nuclear capability—with which it has promised to destroy Israel—the result may well be military engagement either with the United States or a coalition of troops from Europe and the United States.

While today it would be unthinkable for China to provide Iran with troops, naval cover, or the benefit of its nuclear umbrella if Iran were attacked, in the tomorrows that follow, the danger of China coming to the defense of Iran will clearly grow as China's military continues its modernization and buildup and as China's thirst for oil grows. Just imagine China sending one of its own aircraft carriers and several destroyers to patrol the Strait of Hormuz in the Persian Gulf—and possibly confront U.S. naval forces. Just imagine China providing the benefits of its satellite and communication systems to Iran so that it can launch precision-guided missiles at U.S. ships, U.S. troops, or Israeli cities. Just imagine the establishment of Chinese military bases and cadres of military advisers on Iranian soil at the same levels maintained by the United States now in other Middle Eastern countries such as Saudi Arabia and Kuwait.

It is precisely these kind of hot war scenarios in powder kegs, such as the Middle East and emerging areas of conflict in Africa and Latin America, that keep Defense Department analysts up at night in cold sweats.

Trigger 2: Pyongyang—Still Crazy After All These Years

As a charter member of the so-called axis of evil, North Korea's renegade regime of the dictator Kim Jong-Il provides a constant irritant to the United States. It counterfeits millions of dollars in U.S. currency, is a major conduit for the world's drug and arms trades, and periodically threatens South Korea with a blitzkrieg-style invasion that would quickly overrun its capital, Seoul.

North Korea is able to engage in all this rogue behavior precisely because of its ability to hide behind Chinese skirts. China currently provides the Pyongyang regime with two-thirds of its fuel and one-third of its food. In exchange, China is able to exert at least some influence over North Korean policies. Yet, in its dealings with Pyongyang, China remains schizophrenic. On the one hand, it wants the regime to remain in power because it fears Korean unification would bring U.S. troops closer to its borders. On the other hand, China views North Korea in much the same way as the West does, as a loose nuclear cannon with the potential to destabilize the region.

The one certainty in this relationship is its lack of any certainty. This translates into high risk—the proverbial nuclear joker in the deck. Should famine, a dictator's whim, or any number of random events trigger a North Korean military outburst, it would force China to take sides. The result may well be the "Korean War, Part Deux."

Trigger 3: The China-Russia Connection

Just as China has exhibited schizophrenic behavior toward North Korea, its relations with Russia have a similar quality. On the one hand, as noted earlier, China historically has feared—and often fought with—the Russian Bear. On the other hand, the Russian Bear and Chinese Panda seem to be moving much closer together economically, militarily, and strategically.

Economically, China has become one of Russia's most important energy consumers. Militarily, Russia has become one of China's most important suppliers of sophisticated technologies and weaponry. Strategically, Russia and China now regularly conduct joint military operations. This budding Chinese-Russian alliance—once mercifully avoided during the peak of the Cold War era—is rising up to challenge the United States.

Trigger 4: The Rising Sun Versus the Red Star

Economic relations between China and Japan have never been closer. Japan's economy is heavily dependent on its burgeoning trade with China, and China has benefited greatly from importing sophisticated Japanese technologies and management skills.

Even as mutually beneficial economics has united the two countries, cold-steel politics and harsh rhetoric are driving them apart. As one flashpoint and long-festering wound, China continues to object to Japan's revisionist history of the Rape of Nanjing and other Japanese atrocities committed during the 1930s occupation of China. Nor has China ever forgotten that it was a militaristic Japan that once turned Taiwan into a colony in 1895 following the first Sino-Japanese war.

Not coincidentally, Japanese public opinion against China is at a historic low. Anti-Chinese sentiments are being fueled not just by China's repeated attempts to humiliate Japan on what the Japanese consider to be issues that are quite literally dead and buried. The Japanese populace has also been swayed by a number of perceived provocations, not the least of which is Beijing's pivotal role in preventing Japan from gaining a permanent seat on the U.N. Security Council. Japan also rightly fears that once China reaches a higher level of economic development, Japan will become expendable, and China will become a much more dangerous competitor rather than a consumer of Japanese products.

With the United States putting increasing pressure on Japan to remilitarize and provide a counterweight to Chinese influence in the region, this is a hot war trigger very much in the making.

Trigger 5: The Cuban Missile Crisis—Déjà Vu All Over Again

Put this possible hot war trigger in the category of high irony. It would be high irony indeed if the United States were forced to go to the nuclear brink a second time over Cuba because yet another communist superpower had covertly planted nuclear missiles on Cuban soil. This is hardly far-fetched.

China is already using an old Soviet base of operations in Cuba to spy on the United States for both military and commercial purposes. As China develops sophisticated anti-satellite weapons and space war capabilities (discussed in the next chapter), its covert Cuban connection will play an increasingly critical role in China's ability to project global military power. For those who clearly remember the first Cuban missile crisis, the phrase most commonly heard at that time was "only 90 miles away." Cuba as a twenty-first century Chinese enclave and weapons depot is no less a threat to America than Soviet nuclear missiles were in the 1960s.

Trigger 6: "China Si, Yanqui No!"

Cuba is not the only hot war trigger in Latin America—nor the biggest source of current tensions. That source may be found in China's dangerously provocative tango with the populist anti-American president of Venezuela, Hugo Chavez. Even as the United States has sought to impose an arms embargo on Venezuela for its assistance to terrorist regimes, an ever-opportunistic China has stepped into the breach, brazenly trading weapons for oil. As an unrepentant Chavez taunts the United States with threats of turning over some of Venezuela's U.S. F-16 fighter jets to Cuba or Iran, China is orchestrating a Latin American arms buildup of unprecedented proportions.

Underlying these growing tensions is the fact that Venezuela is the fourth-largest supplier of oil to the United States. What is particularly disturbing here is that China has already cut oil exploration deals with Venezuela that over time will significantly reduce the flow of Venezuelan oil to the United States. At some point, America's self-interest as well as its guardianship role in its own hemisphere may motivate the United States to respond.

Trigger 7: Thy Trade War Cup Runneth Over

The Prussian Major General Carl von Clausewitz once famously remarked, "War is merely a continuation of politics." He might well have added that politics is merely a continuation of economics.

In this case, China's emergence as the world's "factory floor" is in many ways a zero-sum game in which the creation of millions of new manufacturing jobs in China have come at the expense of millions of existing manufacturing jobs in the United States and Europe, and in developing countries, such as Bangladesh, Cambodia, and Mexico. That much of China's competitive advantage derives from a set of unfair trade practices has not been lost on world leaders. The result has been increasing trade frictions between China and many other countries now running large trade deficits with China. The result, in turn, has been a growing drumbeat for the world to crack down on the set of China's unfair trade practices identified in Chapter 1, "The Cheating 'China Price' and Weapons of Mass Production." These unfair trade practices include flagrant currency manipulation, illegal export subsidies, rampant counterfeiting and piracy, and environmental, health, and safety standards far below international norms.

To date, China has reacted extremely poorly to these trade frictions. Rather than reform its unfair trade practices, it has erected even higher trade barriers to its own domestic markets. If a quickly escalating retaliatory trade war between China and the rest of the world were to trigger a severe global recession, this economic conflict could quickly mushroom into broader military conflict. That is a lesson the world learned with extreme pain at least once when a trade-war-induced global depression in the 1930s helped trigger World War II.

Trigger 8: China Implodes, the World Explodes

As discussed extensively in Chapter 8, "China's Chaotic 'Wars from Within'—The Dragon Comes Apart at the Seams," China's rapid and unsustainable rate of economic growth is spawning a wide variety of rapidly escalating "wars from within." Plausible wars from within scenarios include the following:

- A severe recession or runaway inflation that mobilizes workers, students, and consumers
- The collapse of a major element of Chinese infrastructure such as the Three Gorges Dam that once again exposes the incompetence of the Chinese bureaucracy
- Yet another major government corruption scandal that accentuates the growing schism between the fat cats of the Communist Party versus the people now suffering rising income disparities
- A failure to stem the tide of defective products and contaminated food now killing or injuring as many people in China as this tide is harming people around the world
- The continued dramatic rise in environmental pollution of China's air basins and waterways and the collateral dramatic rise in cancer rates and heart and lung disease
- The reemergence of SARS or some other type of pandemic that may be traced to China's abject lack of sanitary conditions
- The absence of any affordable and fully functioning health-care or pension system
- A pro-democracy movement to throw off the yoke of totalitarianism

Any one of these wars from within have the potential to be a hot war trigger because of the highly aggressive and confrontational way the Communist Party is most likely to respond to them. As explained by Pentagon analysts:

> At the core of China's overall strategy rests the desire to maintain a continuous rule of the Chinese Communist Party (CCP). A deep-rooted fear of losing political power shapes the leadership's strategic outlook and drives many of its choices. As a substitute for the failure of communist ideology, the CCP has based its legitimacy on the twin pillars of economic performance and nationalism. As a consequence, domestic economic and social difficulties may lead China to

attempt to bolster support by stimulating nationalist sentiment, which could result in more aggressive behavior in
foreign and security affairs than we might otherwise expect.

❖   ❖   ❖   ❖   ❖

These eight possible hot war triggers juxtaposed against China's
rapid military buildup add up to one of the most volatile situations the
world has ever faced. Add to this volatility the possible militarization
and weaponization of space by the Chinese as discussed in the next
chapter and you have a twenty-first century seemingly destined for
conflict—unless we all act soon.

11

Racing for the Ultimate Strategic High Ground—The Coming China Star Wars

If the enemy holds the high ground, you must not ascend and do battle with him.

—Sun Tzu, *The Art of War*

During the Middle Ming Dynasty (circa 1500), a star-crossed Chinese official named Wan Hu attempted to become the world's first astronaut when he constructed a magnificent flying chair outfitted with 47 gunpowder-filled rockets and 2 kites for wings. After a giant explosion at "lift-off," neither the rocket chair nor the daring official was seen again.

Fast forward half a millennium and a now very modern China has traveled light years in its pursuit of the ultimate strategic high ground. A tipping point in that journey into deep space occurred in 2003 when China's first *taikonaut*, Yang Liwei, blasted off from the Jiuquan Satellite Launch Center on a Shenzhou-5 craft.

Today, against the backdrop of an American space program in severe decline, the Chinese National Space Administration is proceeding apace with bold plans for a permanent space station, a mission to Mars, and China's own walk on the moon and eventual moon colony. To support its bold reach for the stars, China continues to rapidly roll out a massive space-related infrastructure. This infrastructure includes a fourth space launch center, a domestically built

military and civilian telecommunications satellite network, a Global
Positioning System (GPS) satellite constellation known as *Beidou,* a
powerful new line of launch vehicles, a fleet of deepwater space-
tracking ships, and ground stations established in Chinese client
nations such as Cuba and Zimbabwe.

China's leaders repeatedly insist they "come in peace" to space.
However, the evidence of the Chinese militarization of space continues to mount. The whole situation is eerily reminiscent of the
famous *Twilight Zone* episode in which aliens arrive on Earth suppos-
edly "to serve man." Only after the aliens depart with their cargo of
human flesh do we learn that "To Serve Man" is the title of the alien's
cookbook.

Given the strategic importance of space, the obvious question
each of us must be asking is this: Will China be friend or foe as it
makes its heavenly ascents? This chapter seeks to answer that question
as it examines the many dimensions of *The Coming China Star Wars.*

The Peaceful Benefits of Space—From Tang to Medical Telemetry

What American wants to go to bed by the light of a
Communist moon?

—President Lyndon Baines Johnson

The U.S. space program was conceived in Cold War fear after the
Soviet launch of Sputnik in 1957, and it is an investment that has
yielded the greatest bounty of peace-time benefits one could ever
imagine. Myriad technical miracles that improve all our lives have
been spun off directly or indirectly from the seemingly purposeless
race to the moon. There is, of course, that most sublime nectar of the
astronaut gods: Tang. There are also these incredible life-enhancing,
life-giving, and life-saving innovations:

- The GPS network
- The World Wide Web, a.k.a. the Internet
- Solar power, fuel cells, and a variety of other alternative energies
- A wealth of new materials, ranging from plastics and insulators to lubricants
- Medical applications from CAT and MRI scans and needle breast biopsies to "medical telemetry" (that is, the monitoring stations you are plugged into at your hospital bed)
- A complex, satellite array of hurricane-, wildfire-, and weather-tracking systems that has saved hundreds of thousands of lives and billions of dollars

China insists it is seeking the same kind of peaceful economic benefits that the United States has been generating. In fact, the head of China's *Chang'e* lunar program has explicitly stated that the Apollo moon effort drove the U.S. tech boom and uses that as a rationale for China going to the moon.

For its part, after walking on the moon, America simply walked away. In contrast, China clearly understands that the moon, together with numerous asteroids, boasts a valuable array of precious metals and raw materials—from gold and platinum to extremely rare metals critical to high-tech manufacturing. Successful mining operations in space would do much to alleviate growing raw material shortages and the pollution associated with resource extraction.

From the Chinese perspective, the even bigger lunar prize in the shorter term may well be realizing the enormous potential of nuclear fusion energy. Unlike the current problematic nuclear fission power plants, fusion energy would truly be "too cheap to meter" as well as clean and safe. An ingredient that physicists believe could bring fusion within reach is Helium 3—an extremely rare isotope thought to be abundant on the moon.

The moon's prodigious energy-producing potential is evident in the words of Ouyang Ziyuan, head of China's space program. He has noted, "Each year, three space shuttle missions could bring enough fuel for all human beings across the world." Ouyang might well have added that the successful development of fusion energy from moon-based materials would be a death blow to the OPEC oil cartel and a magic bullet against global warming.

These kinds of undeniable peaceful benefits of space exploration notwithstanding, there are even greater rewards to be had by any nation that can militarily command the ultimate strategic high ground. That is why it is critical to explore the dark side of China's plans for the moon and beyond.

China's Shot Heard 'Round the Galaxy

China's counterspace program—punctuated by the January 2007 successful test of a direct-ascent anti-satellite weapon—poses dangers to human space flight and puts at risk the assets of all space faring nations.

—U.S. Department of Defense

The United States unquestionably holds the strategic high ground of space today. What is very much in question, however, is who will hold that strategic high ground in the many tomorrows that will follow.

Today, both the U.S. economy and military depend heavily on a complex network of more than 400 orbiting satellites that provide everything from reconnaissance and navigation to communication and information. The crown jewel of this network is the world's only fully functional GPS, the use of which the United States offers for free to the world.

America's GPS system has made it much easier for you and me to get around town; increased the efficiency of routing for ships, planes, and trains; and protected us from hurricanes and tornadoes. GPS systems also provide farmers with precise guidance for everything from field operations and the detection of insect and disease infestations to cultivation and irrigation. All told, the economic benefits from civilian GPS applications alone are rapidly approaching more than $50 billion annually.

America's GPS and its broader U.S. satellite network are even more critical as targeting and guidance instruments for the military. Over the past three decades, satellite-guided precision munitions have proven time and again they can deliver deadly blows to highly specific targets in the midst of populated cities with a greatly reduced impact on civilians.

Using the vantage point of space, the United States has been able to fight a number of wars with decidedly asymmetrical casualties. For example, during the first Gulf War, fewer than 150 Americans died in combat while anywhere from 30,000 to 100,000 Iraqi soldiers were killed. The results were similar in both Kosovo and in the initial invasion campaign for the 2003 Iraq War.

Whatever you might think of these military actions by the United States, the broader strategic point is that the U.S. domination of space has allowed most American troops to stay safely out of harm's way while inflicting massive damage on the enemy. In this way, America's space advantage has lowered the human cost of war by many thousands of American lives. It has also made possible the "United States as world policemen" interventions the American public might not have otherwise tolerated.

The "game-changing" domination of space by the Americans has not gone unnoticed by China. In fact, the 1991 Gulf War was an epiphany for Chinese strategists because it graphically demonstrated that U.S. space superiority completely undermines their long-held tactic of "human wave" troop strength. As Air Force General Thomas Moorman has put it, "Desert Storm was a watershed event in military space applications because, for the first time, space systems were both integral to the conflict and critical to the outcome of the war."

From the Chinese perspective, there are at least two ways to counter the U.S. space advantage. One way is to render the U.S. satellite surveillance system "deaf, dumb, and blind." The other way is to quite literally seize the highest strategic ground in space. That China is developing capabilities in both areas should be evident to anyone who bothers to look.

A New Type of Chinese Junk Sails into Space

Consider China's efforts to develop the capability to neutralize or destroy the U.S. satellite surveillance system. In January 2007, in a shot heard 'round the galaxy, China made it abundantly clear that it fully intends to develop anti-satellite weapons capabilities to challenge U.S. supremacy in space. The details of China's anti-satellite weapons test—that may be rightly described as the single most irresponsible act of space weapons development ever perpetrated by any nation—are interesting in and of themselves.

The satellite the Chinese shot out of the sky was their own Fengyun-1C. This steadfast satellite had dutifully followed its orbit at 537 miles above the Earth for 10 years—circling the globe several times a day from north to south and north again as the world turned beneath its gaze.

On a Thursday morning in January 2007, Fengyun-1C came over the horizon and faithfully transmitted its usual batch of weather data to its home country. About that time, a modified intercontinental ballistic missile lifted off from the Xichang launch facility in Sichuan Province and threw a "kinetic kill vehicle" onto a collision course with the innocent weather satellite. Upon impact, the nuts, bolts, panels, and wires of the satellite, together with thousands of fragments and pieces of the kinetic kill vehicle, were scattered into a massive cloud of debris. The resultant field of Chinese space junk has quickly become a huge navigational hazard for the vast majority of satellites.

As Nicholas Johnson, NASA's Chief Scientist for Orbital Debris, has described the dangers:

> [China's] debris cloud extends from less than 125 miles to more than 2,292 miles, encompassing all of low Earth orbit. The majority of the debris have mean altitudes of 528 miles or greater, which means most will be very long-lived. ... Any of this debris has the potential for seriously disrupting or terminating the mission of operational spacecraft in low Earth orbit. This satellite breakup represents the most prolific and serious fragmentation in the course of 50 years of space operations.

At the time, many pundits and politicians would ask: What quite literally "on earth" would possess a developing nation desperately seeking international approval to pull such a dangerous stunt and risk such geopolitical fallout? Given the Chinese government's lack of transparency, there really is no satisfactory answer to that question. Perhaps even more chilling, immediately after the event, Chinese diplomats and political leaders seemed as surprised as the rest of the world by this test!

In fact, China's civilian leaders were unable to describe the test or offer a coordinated explanation for several days. One alarming possibility is that the People's Liberation Army and its own rogue cadre of space hawks may have conducted this test without full disclosure to the politicians as a demonstration of their strength.

Regardless of whether China's anti-satellite weapons test was a renegade act by the military or a cold calculation by the political leadership, the North American Aerospace Defense Command continues to track more than 2,000 of the larger pieces of the late Fengyun-1C at altitudes ranging from 125 to 2,500 miles. These pieces have begun to stretch out along the doomed satellite's inertial path. As the Fengyun-1C was in a "sun synchronous" orbit—circling the Earth from pole to pole—it has saddled the Earth with a small Saturn-like ring of trash running from north to south.

As noted previously, this trash poses a grave threat to all nations seeking to explore space—including the Chinese. The reason is that most satellites and all manned space missions travel in more nearly equatorial orbits—circling the Earth from east to west—and are therefore forced to traverse the Chinese obstacle course in space several times a day. In fact, more than two-thirds of all the nearly 3,000 craft in orbit are at risk of disastrous collisions with this material, and the list of potential victims includes the International Space Station and its crew.

On top of this, every remaining U.S. Space Shuttle mission, with its delicate and all too fragile outer armor, will have to fly through China's ring of deadly space junk several times. Special care will have to be taken to avoid the larger tracked chunks, but many tens of thousands of smaller, yet deadly, pieces may go undetected. Because these pieces are traveling at speeds of more than 18,000 miles per hour in an orbit roughly perpendicular to the path of the endangered satellites, the speed of impact is much higher than with most space debris that is traveling on the same general trajectory as the satellites themselves.

Of Would-Be Chinese Tojos and Bringing America to Its Knees

For countries that can never win a war with the United States by using the method of tanks and planes, attacking the U.S. space system may be an irresistible and most tempting choice.

—Wang Hucheng, Chinese military analyst

What specifically are the dangers posed by China's development of an anti-satellite weapons capability? Consider just the vulnerability of the American GPS system. It was designed for 30 satellites in 6 orbital planes, with each orbital plane requiring 4 functional units as a minimum for full service to military and civilian users. A Chinese attack that disabled a mere dozen of these units would effectively result in a system failure.

As bizarre and irresponsible as China's anti-satellite weapon (ASAT) test was, its arsenal of kinetic kill vehicles that can literally knock a satellite out of space is but one component of a more complete counterspace program that China's People's Liberation Army has been aggressively pursuing in recent years. Indeed, China also has been covertly testing high-energy ground-based lasers capable of temporarily blinding satellites. *Jane's Defence Weekly* reports that such lasers have already been successfully used against U.S. spy satellites over China. Submarine-mounted lasers that can literally melt the optical systems of satellites are also under development along with radio jammers directed at GPS satellite signals and plasma-based weaponry that can damage satellites using electromagnetic pulses.

This is all very serious business because a Chinese attack on optical and radar surveillance satellites could degrade U.S. capabilities far beyond China. For example, the loss of geosynchronous and medium Earth orbit satellites could disrupt American military communications from Afghanistan and Iraq to Guam. Hits on several GPS satellites could render the entire system militarily unusable and cause serious economic damage to commercial users, too.

At greatest immediate risk from China's satellite killers is Taiwan. For years, the Chinese military has spent the largest portion of its budget and training time preparing to retake the "renegade province." To date, U.S. air and naval forces have had to demonstrate American support for Taiwan three times—in the first Taiwan Strait Crisis in 1954–55, during a second conflict in 1958, and the third time in 1995–96 when the U.S.S. *Nimitz* super aircraft carrier passed through the strait as a show of strength while China was firing "test missiles" dangerously close to Taiwan.

China's new satellite killers dramatically change the battlefield. Would-be Chinese Tojos within the hawkish wing of the People's Liberation Army can now credibly argue that a Pearl Harbor–like, preemptive strike on U.S. satellites would impair U.S. forces to a degree that would preclude swift U.S. action in the Taiwan Strait. In this hawkish view, a defanged America will have learned its lesson about interfering in Chinese affairs, while a large number of other countries aligned more with China would surely applaud the removal of "arrogant U.S. astro-hegemony."

Lest anyone think that such a scenario is improbable, consider that Chinese strategists have specifically called for this scenario. Borrowing from the American playbook, they have labeled such an attack "Space Shock and Awe" and argued that such an attack must be devastating enough to deter any further American military action in a crisis and "bring the opponent to his knees."

China's GPS—Simply Redundant or Incredibly Dangerous?

China has developed the Beidou system for both military and civilian uses. In this regard, China is following the lead of the United States in developing a system that is at its core a military system, but will also serve a variety of civil and commercial applications. The main concern for Chinese is that GPS can be turned off or degraded by the United States in the event of conflict. Consequently, China's national interests require access to a satellite navigation and positioning system that is independent of foreign operation.

—*China Brief*

Beidou is the Chinese name for the constellation commonly known to Westerners as the Big Dipper. The tail of the big dipper has long been used by northern latitude sailors to locate Polaris, the North Star, the most important celestial landmark for navigation.

China's first-generation *Beidou* system will use four geosynchronous satellites and is projected to be online by 2008. The second-generation Beidou 2 system will utilize five geosynchronous satellites and 30 low Earth orbit satellites. Beidou 1 alone will provide coverage in the Asian theater to an accuracy of approximately 10 yards.

Both Chinese politicians and military leaders see the *Beidou* system as essential to safeguard China's own territory, assert itself as a regional power in Asia, and ensure its right of access to resources around the globe—from Persian Gulf oil and African precious metals to Brazilian iron ore and Cuban nickel. There are at least four reasons why the primary purpose of Beidou is ultimately to wage war.

First, the U.S. GPS system works very well in China. It is fully available at no charge to Chinese civilian, government, and commercial users. Thus, for peaceful applications, Beidou is clearly a redundant, high cost luxury.

Second, China argues that its own system will be technically superior to America's. However, given China's technical lag, an improvement in accuracy is unlikely and economically unjustifiable.

Third, China argues that it needs a backup to the U.S. system in case it fails. However, the only really likely cause of failure would be an attack by another nation, most likely China.

Fourth, the only time that the United States would ever disable Chinese access to the system would be in time of war. That's why China is also preparing to utilize the Russian's Glonass GPS system currently being deployed while investing 200 million euros in the European Galileo GPS project.

The broader point is this: With a proven, free U.S. solution and Russian and European backups in production, the primary purpose of *Beidou* is for the support of offensive military applications and the use of precision-guided weaponry that might be so distasteful that all three GPS providers—the United States, Russia, and Europe—would shut China down.

It is critical to note here that the wedding of China's *Beidou* GPS system to its ever-increasing array of sophisticated weaponry poses an additional threat that reaches far beyond any possible military conflict between China and the United States over, for example, Taiwan. This threat relates to the sale of highly accurate missiles to rogue nations around the world.

Consider the Middle East. When the United States invaded Iraq in 1991, Saddam Hussein lobbed Scud missiles toward Israeli cities. Although these highly inaccurate weapons resulted in few casualties, it would be another thing entirely for Iran or Syria to buy from the Chinese weapons bazaar the capability to accurately hit Jewish population centers, government buildings, Israeli troops, and military installations. In this vein, it should also be noted that Chinese-supplied munitions routinely find their way from Iran to Hezbollah forces in Lebanon for use against Israel.

When Sci-Fi Becomes Sci-Fact—From Rail Guns to Rocks in Space

The pursuit of science, despite its social benefits, is not a social virtue; its practitioners can be men so self-centered as to be lacking in social responsibility.

—Robert Heinlein

While China's development of anti-satellite weapons capabilities and its own GPS system are clearly designed to neutralize or destroy America's current superiority in space, the deployment of nuclear and other weapons in space is another matter entirely. Indeed, it is a grotesque and ultimate escalation of the nuclear arms race that continues to be conducted on planet Earth. That said, "nukes in space" might not even be necessary as an ultimate space weapon. In this regard, the science fiction novels of the last century are surprisingly enlightening.

Consider Robert Heinlein's 1966 novel *The Moon is a Harsh Mistress*. Its central plot line graphically illustrates the insurmountable advantage of being at the top of a "gravity well"—the space equivalent of holding the high ground. Heinlein's "heroes" are convicts on a lunar penal colony who revolt and then bring the nations of the world to a standstill by simply flinging huge stones off the moon's surface with a magnetic accelerator. The boulders falling 250,000 miles to the Earth's surface arrive with a force equivalent to a nuclear warhead.

Fast forward to the twenty-first century and the concept of "rocks in space" is no longer science fiction. Today, manmade "asteroids of doom" can easily and cheaply obliterate any facility or city on Earth. The so-called rail gun, or electromagnetic gun, technology to do this already exists, and it is relatively simple to set up. Nor can such magnetic accelerators simply be declared violations of the 1967 Outer Space Treaty, because they are "dual-use" technologies—that is, they are very handy for lobbing not just weapons but also raw materials to assembly stations in orbit.

America's hands are certainly not clean on the "rocks in space" issue. The U.S. Air Force is working on a project to launch small payloads into Earth orbit with a large rail gun, and NASA has plans for such devices at its planned lunar base. In addition, the U.S. Navy will be deploying electromagnetic gun-based artillery on ships by 2010.

It also should be noted here that, unlike nuclear weapons, rocks require no dangerous materials to mine, process, or store and have no delicate electronic guidance or detonation systems to disable. They are cheap, reliable, and virtually foolproof against all the ballistic and laser defense systems the United States has developed for dealing with Chinese intercontinental ballistic missiles (ICBMs). Finally, while the target city or installation is nicely obliterated, there is none of that messy radioactive fallout to upset environmentalists in neighboring countries.

China's Nukes in Space and the Assassin's Mace

We Chinese will prepare ourselves for the destruction of all of the cities east of Xian [in central China]. Of course, the Americans will have to be prepared that hundreds of their cities will be destroyed by the Chinese.

—Major General Zhu Chenghu, People's Liberation Army

Many peace-loving people in Europe and the United States find it hard to imagine that China—or any other country for that matter—would actually deploy offensive nuclear weapons in space. This would be a clear violation of the world's international space treaty as well as an affront to all human decency. However, since the days of Sun Tzu, deception has been a Chinese military strategy of choice—a strategy designed to surprise potential enemies and force them into an immediate surrender with minimal conflict.

That this is a legitimate concern is evident in the writings of two colonels from China's National Defense University, both of whom are active officers in the People's Liberation Army. For his part, Colonel Jai Junming in his 2002 book, *Space Operations*, has strongly advocated building offensive space weapons platforms that he refers to as "assassin's maces." Colonel Li Daguang has similarly urged the People's Liberation Army to develop both defensive and *offensive* weapons in space.

It would certainly be reassuring to imagine that these Chinese officers are simply academic daydreamers exploring far beyond the boundaries of actual Chinese military policy and thought. However, similar statements from Chinese military analysts accurately foreshadowed China's kinetic kill vehicle ASAT test in 2007.

As for concerns about China's possible "nukes in space," many experts have suggested that China's ambitious manned space program is a thinly veiled dual-use military platform. Supporting this contention is the fact that each secretive Shenzhou spacecraft is fully capable of leaving behind an 8 foot by 9 foot orbital module that contains a nuclear bomb.

Again, the words of Colonel Li Daguang are instructive regarding the secretive nature of such a deployment: "Considering certain constraints from the international society, the construction of such a unit should be carried out secretly by keeping a low profile."

Should China secretly and successfully deploy a string of nuclear weapons in space, these space swords of Damocles would be ready to drop on American targets with virtually no notice. Unlike ICBMs that are launched from land or sea by powerful rockets, orbital warheads could simply be "nudged" down with no telltale boost-phase infrared flare. Already at the top of their trajectory, they avoid a slow ascent phase and arrive on target quickly and probably quite unexpectedly. Consequently, they would be virtually unstoppable by existing American, European, Russian, or Israeli missile defense systems.

Again, for the doubters, there are the words of another one of China's own military strategists, Zhao Ruian. Zhao strongly advocates a multi-role orbital A-bomb. This "new-concept strategic ballistic missile" would be "a multi-task, multi-role attack weapon capable of implementing random orbit transfer from Earth orbits and can serve the function of an intercontinental ballistic missile, an anti-satellite weapon, and an orbital bomber weapon."

Evolution Roars into Space—The Ultimate Survival of the Species

The overriding reason to establish a colony on the moon is humanity's survival: Darwin achieves liftoff.

—William E. Burroughs

The threats that China may pose strategically and militarily notwithstanding, there is a final major compelling reason why China is reaching for the stars. This is a reason that not only lies at the very core of *The Coming China Star Wars* but also speaks to the ultimate survival of the species *and* under which political system the human species will live.

Long before economics was declared the "dismal science" by English historian Thomas Carlyle—and ever since—experts have been warning of impending doom. The end may come by overpopulation, resource depletion, economic failure, nuclear war, some high-tech biodisaster, or environmental depredation.

Each of these disaster scenarios (and most others) depend on the basic Malthusian theme that the human race, which has evolved to compete ferociously for resources, is trapped on a planet growing too small to support its rapidly expanding population. Like too many rats breeding in a cage, the end result is destined to be a truly ugly one.

Buzz Aldrin, the second man to step on the moon, and John Barnes make the point clearly in their sci-fi novel *Encounter With Tiber*: "There's not a place in the universe that's safe forever; the universe is telling us, 'Spread out, or wait around and die.'"

Regardless of which doomsday scenario you might worry about, each can be neatly resolved by opening up human migration to the moon, space stations, and other solar bodies. From this perspective, the Earth could benefit in much the same way that Dickensian England did. This small island country once featured "dark satanic mills" and cruel and crushing work conditions not unlike in today's China. However, England was at least partly transformed back into a "green and pleasant land" through the growth of Britannia's overseas colonies, which had the corresponding benefits of a safety valve for overpopulation and access to global resources and trade. Today, the colonization of space offers precisely the same virtues.

In fact, space exploration gives us a golden opportunity to expand in a nonconfrontational manner for the first time since the first humans crossed the Bering Land Bridge into North America some 15,000 to 20,000 years ago. This land bridge, which existed over the Bering Strait during the ice ages, allowed these first discoveries of the Americas to behold an unspoiled continent of vast riches. Through this Darwinian lens, the ongoing evolutionary conflict on Earth between various countries, religions, and political ideologies is about to approach a literal quantum leap in the selection process.

One of the "fish"—likely the United States, China, or Russia—is going to crawl out onto the shore, and the others will be left behind in the muddy pond. The question is which society and political organization will be representing humanity in the cosmos? To frame the question another way, do we want a human diaspora based on diversity, tolerance, and the Jeffersonian ideals of liberty? Or, do we want an amoral, neo-Maoist vision from China's central planners?

12

How to Fight and Win
the Coming China Wars!

Unless strong actions are taken now both by China and the rest of the world, The Coming China Wars *are destined to be fought over everything from decent jobs, livable wages, and leading-edge technologies to strategic resources such as oil, copper, and steel, and eventually to our most basic of all needs—bread, water, and air.*

—Introduction to *The Coming China Wars*

No problem can be solved until it is clearly understood. What should be clearly understood as this book comes to its close are these essential truths:

- China's hyper-rate of economic growth is export driven and ultimately unsustainable.
- China has been able to conquer one export market after another and emerge as the world's "factory floor" because it "cheats" in the international trading arena using its "China Price" advantage.
- The cheating China Price relies on an extensive array of unfair, mercantilist trade practices, including a wide range of illegal export subsidies, rampant counterfeiting and piracy, and flagrant currency manipulation.

- China's unfair trade practices also feature environmental, health, and safety standards that are so lax and so weakly enforced that they have made China the most polluted country in the world as well as the most dangerous place to work.
- Because of the economic consequences and environmental "fallout" from China's export-driven growth and the "zero-sum" nature of this growth, the citizens of America, the countries of Europe, and all countries running large trade deficits with China ultimately pay dearly for cheap Chinese goods with a loss of jobs, stagnant wages, skyrocketing energy prices, unsafe products, a loss of political sovereignty, increased global warming, and a more polluted world.

These essential truths inevitably lead to a compelling need to address a question that is so critical to ensuring a prosperous and peaceful twenty-first century: What can be done to fight—and win—*The Coming China Wars*?

A New "Made in China" Consumer Calculus

The first line of defense in any *China Wars* strategy must start with a radical change in consumer behavior. I do not, however, urge any consumer to simply "boycott Chinese products." That is a Draconian prescription. For many products, it is also impractical. I do, however, emphatically urge every consumer to do the following:

- Question whether you really need what you are about to buy from China.
- Carefully consider the *hidden costs* associated with buying Chinese products, not just China's cheap prices, and factor the hidden costs of a world "Made in China" into your buying decisions.

If this book has done anything, it has carefully identified a wide range of the hidden costs of buying what, in reality, are not so "cheap" Chinese goods. These hidden costs include job destruction, stagnant wages, rapidly rising food and fuel costs, a dirtier and hotter planet, tacit support for Chinese repression, the inadvertent funding of China's military buildup, and a collateral dramatic increase in geopolitical risks around the world.

To increase the range of "Not Made in China" alternatives, we as consumers also have an important role to play:

- Send emails, postcards, or letters to retailers and manufacturers letting them know you want non-China options. This works! For example, in response to consumer demand, Wal-Mart has increased its floor space for "Made in USA" products such as Tramontina's new line of cookware and thereby created new manufacturing jobs in Tramontina's Wisconsin factory.

- Let retailers and manufacturers also know what you *didn't* buy. Tell them that you did not purchase a particular product or products because it was made in China and that you were concerned about product quality, the environment, jobs, or some other issue.

Finally, to protect yourself and your family from the flood of contaminated, defective, and cancerous products now coming out of China, as an informed consumer, you should

- Seek out websites such as www.notmadeinchina.net, www.madeinusa.org, and other consumer advocacy sources that provide information about "Not Made in China" alternatives.

- Lobby your elected officials for better product labeling so that finished products that are not made in China but which nonetheless have substantial Chinese components can be identified.

- Regularly check the websites of organizations such as the U.S. Consumer Product Safety Commission for the latest recalls and safety news at www.cpsc.gov.

What Voters Must Do

Although changing our individual consumer behavior is an essential part of solving our "Made in China" problems, we as *voters* have an equally important role to play. This is because any ultimate victory in *The Coming China Wars* depends on the swift adoption of the comprehensive government policy actions that I will describe in this chapter. However, none of the necessary prescriptive actions will ever be taken unless we as voters exert much stronger pressure on our political leaders than we have to date.

In this regard, I must be very candid: To date, we as voters have simply not done our job in making China a pivotal electoral issue. One major reason for voter apathy is the narcotic effect that cheap Chinese goods have had on us.

A second major reason, particularly in the United States, is America's preoccupation with the Middle East. As a result of America's singular focus on Iraq, the longer term and potentially even more dangerous threats posed by China have been largely ignored.

Still a third major reason for the lack of political action, which this book has specifically sought to address, is a general lack of awareness of the far-ranging implications of a world increasingly "Made in China."

As a result of these political factors, both the United States and Europe lack a comprehensive set of China policies. This is despite *huge* trade imbalances. That's why we as informed voters must now speak up in the loudest possible voices and let our political representatives know that the time for action is long overdue. These steps are absolutely critical:

- Write your elected representatives, relevant government agencies, and all political candidates seeking your vote, and urge them to aggressively and comprehensively address the China problem along the lines of the policy prescriptions offered here.
- Get involved with your political party and work hard to get a "China plank" in your party's platform.

- Help spread the word! Give your copy of *The Coming China Wars* to a friend, or donate your copy to your local library.

What Our Governments Must Do

Just exactly which prescriptive policy actions should our government take? The first and most important action is the adoption of a comprehensive framework to ensure that all trade with China is not just free trade but also fair trade.

To avoid any direct confrontation with China—and a possible trade war—this comprehensive framework need not mention China by name. The purpose of the framework should be to specify a set of inviolable rules and sanctions that would make it impossible for any country to engage in the kind of unfair trading practices now common to China.

Here's a specific example of such an omnibus trade bill as it has been tailored for passage by the American Congress:

- Any country wishing to engage in free and fair trade with the United States must refrain from the use of illegal export subsidies or currency manipulation and abide by the rules of the World Trade Organization.
- Any U.S. trading partner must also respect intellectual property; adopt and enforce health, safety, and environmental regulations consistent with U.S. and international norms; provide decent wages and working conditions; and ban the use of slave labor.
- Any U.S. trading partner that fails to abide by these rules shall be subject to all appropriate actions and sanctions necessary to ensure both free and fair trade.

One major political obstacle to the successful adoption of such an omnibus trade bill is the mistaken perception in some quarters that any attempt to crack down on China's mercantilist practices is "protectionist." Defending one's country and its consumers, businesses, and workers against unfair trading practices is not protectionist but rather simply common sense.

As a final point, one of the most astute, influential, and compelling voices on America's particular China problem is the U.S.-China Commission. To fight back against one of the worst features of Chinese mercantilism, this commission has urged Congress to

- Enact legislation to define currency manipulation as an illegal export subsidy and allow the subsidy to be taken into account when determining penalty tariffs.
- Amend the law to allow currency manipulation to be added to other prohibited subsidies when calculating anti-dumping and countervailing duty penalties.
- Eliminate the requirement that the Department of the Treasury first determine whether a country intends to gain an export advantage before deciding that country has manipulated its currency.

The U.S.-China Commission also recommends that the U.S. government bring a case before the World Trade Organization that identifies suppression of labor rights in China as an unfair trade practice.

Zero Tolerance for Chinese Counterfeiting and Piracy

As illustrated in Chapter 2, "China's Counterfeit Economy and Not-So-Swashbuckling Pirates," China is unlikely to unilaterally clamp down on its rampant counterfeiting and piracy because these illegal activities create tens of millions of jobs in China. That's why in addition to attacking intellectual property theft in an omnibus trade bill, the United States, Europe, and other countries around the world should

- Adopt a "zero-tolerance" policy toward counterfeiting and piracy; prosecute to the fullest extent of the law anyone who knowingly sells or distributes illegal pirated or counterfeit goods; and confiscate and destroy all such goods.

- Tighten border security to more effectively interdict pirated and counterfeit goods. This action will synergistically serve other goals such as reducing the risk of terrorist attacks.

In addition, to directly address one of the most dangerous aspects of Chinese counterfeiting, the sale and distribution of fake prescription drugs in retail stores and over the Internet, our government should:

- Run regular sting operations to detect Internet fraud involving fake pharmaceuticals.
- Criminally prosecute as a felony anyone who knowingly sells and distributes fake pharmaceuticals and impose appropriate fines and jail time.
- Require all websites to prominently display their country of origin to prevent Chinese scam artists from masquerading as Canadian or U.S. pharmacies.
- Notify credit card companies and organizations such as Mastercard and PayPal of any possible illegal Internet activities so they can withdraw their services from the questionable websites.
- Immediately shut down any website found to be selling fake pharmaceuticals.

Protecting Our Food, Drug, and Product Supply Chain

As documented in Chapter 3, "'Made in China'—The Ultimate Warning Label," the world is now subject to a flood of cancerous, contaminated, and defective products from China. From that chapter, it should be equally clear that the Chinese regulatory system is totally incapable of policing this dangerous problem. That's why governments around the world must:

- Significantly increase the regulatory budgets of government agencies such as America's Food and Drug Administration so that imports can be adequately inspected.

- Ensure more complete product labeling so that finished products that are not made in China but that nonetheless have substantial Chinese components can be clearly identified by consumers.

- Pass legislation that will make it much easier to hold companies financially and legally accountable for selling foreign products that can harm or kill people or pets.

End the Blood-for-Oil Wars

As this book has illustrated, many of the conflicts between China and the rest of the world—from Africa and the Middle East to Latin America—involve fights over access to oil and natural gas reserves and other resources. This is particularly true when it comes to China-U.S. relations. That's why both the U.S. and Europe must make:

- A firm programmatic commitment to greater energy conservation, efficiency, independence, and domestic production.

- Any such program must recognize the urgency of the matter and therefore be on the scale and accelerated timeline of the Manhattan Project, which yielded the atomic bomb to end World War II, and the Apollo Program, which led to America's walk on the moon.

Increasing energy efficiency would synergistically serve numerous other goals, particularly slowing the process of global warming. Major technological spin-offs, such as those that America got from its space program, would also surely result from the significant investments in science and engineering education required to achieve this goal.

Expose China's "Veto Abuse," Counter Chinese Imperialism

Despite increasing criticism, China continues to regularly and crassly trade the power of its U.N. veto in exchange for energy, raw materials, and access to markets. The results thus far have been the slaughter or rape of millions in Darfur, unconscionable diplomatic cover for a rogue Iran, and the shielding of corrupt, totalitarian African political leaders everywhere from Angola to Zimbabwe. Accordingly:

- American and European leaders should publicly condemn China in no uncertain terms for its crass commercial use of its U.N. veto and make it clear that if China wants to enjoy all of the benefits of an international marketplace, it must act responsibly.

- If China continues its amoral behavior, American and European leaders should move to strip China of its status as a permanent member of the U.N. Security Council. Whereas successfully stripping China of its veto would be highly unlikely, the symbolic act of debating the issue might be enough to change Chinese behavior.

While China's crass commercial use of its U.N. veto is a straightforward issue, Chinese imperialism in Africa and Latin America is a much more complex problem. As illustrated in Chapter 5, "The World's Most Ironic Imperialist and Weapons of Mass Construction," China has simply been much more effective than all other nations in creating grassroots economic, financial, and political ties with developing countries as part of its coordinated campaign to gain control of the raw materials and natural resources China needs to feed its industrial machine.

Some of the ways Chinese imperialism may be countered by the United States have been suggested by Joshua Kurlantzick in his book *Charm Offensive*, which analyzes the projection of China's influence or "soft power" around the world. Kurlantzick's recommendations focus primarily on rebuilding America's diplomatic infrastructure at the grassroots:

- At the top level of the diplomatic pyramid, the president should appoint a public diplomacy czar, preferably an internationally famous figure like Colin Powell or Bill Clinton. This czar should reach out not only to elites abroad but also the larger segments of foreign populations.

- To monitor Chinese activities in any given country, the United States should have one person in each embassy examining that nation's bilateral relations with China—China's aid policies, investment, and public diplomacy as well as Chinese leaders' visits. This will help build up a core of China specialists.

- Increase, don't cut, the budgets of programs like the Voice of America and American Centers offering library facilities and cultural programming in foreign countries.

- Most broadly, China woos countries by bringing its cabinet-level officials on regular trips to nations. This leverages even minor cabinet members to boost relations. The United States should use the same strategy, making sure everyone from the secretaries of agriculture and commerce to the U.S. trade representative devote as much face time to Asia, Latin America, and Africa as they currently do to Europe.

In addition to these recommendations, there is this problem: Americans in particular continue to be a very parochial people with little international perspective. This problem begins early on in the U.S. educational system. Indeed, what languages and cultures U.S. children study continue to focus largely on Europe—Spanish, French, and German—to the neglect of Asia. That's why:

- All parents in the United States should urge their school boards to offer and require more courses in Asian languages and international issues.

- U.S. colleges and universities must incorporate a more international perspective to catch up to their European and Asian counterparts.

- Finally, the U.S. government would do well to enlist U.S. companies and philanthropic organizations operating abroad in an active effort to improve the street-level perception of the United States where they do their work. For a country that is as giving in foreign aid as the United States, it gets surprisingly little credit for its largess.

Clean the Skies, Cool the Earth

As documented in Chapter 6, "The Global Warming Wars—Killing Us (and Them) Softly with Their Coal," and in Chapter 7, "The Damnable Dam and Water Wars—Nary a (Clean) Drop to Drink," China's heavy manufacturing model has turned China into the most polluted country in the world as well as the biggest global warmer. These chapters also illustrate that "what happens in China doesn't stay in China." Much of the acid rain in Japan and South Korea is "Made in China," and Chinese smog now regularly hitchhikes on the jetstream over to despoil North American skies. Accordingly:

- All bilateral and multilateral trade agreements should include strong provisions for environmental protection to prevent the kind of "race to the environmental bottom" we are now witnessing in China. By adopting and enforcing such standards in a free-trade framework, all nations of the world, not just China, would be forced to compete on a level playing field. The environment and people's health would be much better for it.

On the global-warming front, former Vice President and Nobel Laureate Al Gore has been transformed by an avalanche of scientific facts from a left-wing crazy to the planet's most authoritative political voice on the subject. At present, the two biggest obstacles to fighting global warming are the world's two biggest carbon dioxide emitters—China and the United States—while a rapidly industrializing India also must share part of the blame.

Regrettably, neither China nor India has shown any willingness to sign a truly meaningful global warming treaty with any teeth. For its part, the United States has used inaction by China and India as its own excuse not to act aggressively on the global-warming issue for fear of losing further competitive advantage in world manufacturing markets to these rising rivals.

That said, there is a simple and direct way for the U.S. Congress and president to address the global-warming issue in a way that would significantly improve, rather than degrade, American manufacturing competitiveness:

- Agree to stringent carbon controls in an international global-warming framework and then pass legislation that levies a tax on the carbon content of all domestic manufactured goods as well as foreign imported goods. Because the United States is much more energy efficient than China and India, such a carbon tax would be much higher for countries such as China and India and therefore a great boon to American manufacturing, American workers, and the global environment.

These recommendations by the U.S.-China Commission should also be promptly adopted:

- Increase the monitoring of air quality in the western United States and support efforts to determine how much of the pollution in the United States can be traced to China.
- Encourage the sale to China of U.S. clean-energy and energy-efficient technologies and the implementation of those technologies in China.
- Encourage the Chinese to adopt nonpolluting energy sources and technologies and apply technologies to fight global warming, such as carbon-capture and carbon-sequestration techniques that prevent carbon dioxide emissions from being released into the atmosphere.

Breaking Out of the World's Largest Prison

As detailed in Chapter 9, "Inside the World's Biggest Prison with Yahoo! the Stool Pigeon and Comrade Orwell," China is the world's biggest prison and ruthlessly cracks down on any type of dissent. The sad fact is that many American companies—from Cisco and Microsoft to Google, Yahoo!, and Skype—have helped construct the "Great Firewall of China" and routinely help China keep the boot to the neck of its people.

On this issue, there is a not so very fine line between meddling in the internal affairs of a country such as China and contributing to Chinese repression through actions and inactions. One step recommended by the U.S.-China Commission that walks a moderate path would be to:

- Increase funding for the Broadcasting Board of Governors' radio, television, and Internet news broadcasts to the people of China. This increased funding would enable these broadcasts to be expanded and to reach a greater proportion of China's population despite jamming and other censoring methods employed by the Chinese government.

A still stronger set of measures would be to:

- Prohibit U.S. companies from disclosing to the Chinese government information about Chinese users or authors of online content.
- Require all U.S. companies that are compelled to take such actions by the Chinese government to inform the U.S. government of its actions and the Chinese government's basis for compelling it to take those actions.
- Prohibit all U.S. companies from directly providing infrastructure and assistance to Chinese censors.

Containing China's Military Threat

In thinking about how to contain an increasingly militaristic China, it is useful to remind ourselves that China's rapid military buildup is being largely financed by American and European consumers who continue to load up on all things made in China. The resultant billions of "Wal-Mart dollars" sent off to China are now being used to radically modernize the People's Liberation Army, buy lethal nuclear submarines and aircraft carriers for the Chinese navy, and finance the purchase of sophisticated Russian aircraft for the Chinese air force. Accordingly:

- It is critical for the United States and Europe to crack down on Chinese unfair trade practices not just from an economic point of view but also from a military and strategic point of view.

Even as the Chinese military is modernizing, the U.S. military is in a significant decline. The wars in Iraq and Afghanistan have taken a very heavy toll on U.S. military readiness and effective troop strength while America's arsenals are growing increasingly depleted. It follows from these observations that in an age where America's military is stretched exceedingly thin, the U.S. government should

- Engage in military interventions only in areas of real U.S. strategic interest where a quick and successful outcome is predictable. Short and effective demonstrations of U.S. military superiority create credibility that often eliminates the need for military action in later conflicts. In contrast, protracted difficult engagements such as the Iraqi campaign undermine this credibility and attract additional opponents that literally smell the blood of a distracted and worn-down superpower.

- Openly question China's need for a growing nuclear arsenal now targeting the major cities of its largest trading partner. (What a sick relationship this is where American toy dollars go to funding Chinese missiles aimed at Chicago, Los Angeles, and San Francisco.)

- Treat the "hot war trigger" Taiwan issue with at least the same respect America has given to the perennial Israeli-Palestinian conflict. Host a summit on the issue and show the Chinese that while America is a firm ally of Taiwan, the United States can also be a valuable "honest broker" when it comes to addressing China's most important foreign policy concern.

Resolution of the Taiwan question in favor of an enduring peace with China would ultimately be far more important to U.S. long-term interests than peace in the Middle East. Moreover, such a rapprochement is probably more attainable in our lifetime. In contrast, failure to resolve the Taiwan question will almost surely result in conflict—and a possible nuclear conflict at that.

To address China's increasing emphasis on asymmetrical warfare, the United States should publicly confront, and refuse to tolerate, Chinese ongoing "test attacks" on U.S. military computer and satellite systems. In addition, the U.S.-China Commission also recommends that Congress:

- Increase funding for military, intelligence, and homeland security programs that monitor and protect American computer networks from damage caused by cyber-attacks.
- Engage China in a military dialogue on the laws of warfare, and specifically how the laws of warfare apply to the cyber and space domains.

Still another important dimension to China's military buildup is China's growing ability to acquire sensitive defense industry technologies. In some cases, these technologies are acquired through highly sophisticated industrial espionage programs—China's spying is the most extensive in the world. In other cases, the defense-related technologies being acquired are "dual-use" technologies that can often be transferred by American corporations in the course of offshoring their production to China. This type of technology transfer can happen quite unwittingly. More often than not, however, in a clear violation of World Trade Organization rules, American companies are being forced to transfer their technologies to China as a condition of market entrant.

To help prevent such technology transfers, the U.S.-China Commission strongly recommends that Congress:

- Increase funding for U.S. government efforts to detect and prevent illicit technology transfers to China.
- Provide regular reports on the how the research and development now being conducted by U.S. companies in China might be adapted to military applications.

Finally, the U.S. Congress, the Departments of Commerce and Defense, and the U.S. Trade representative should work together to:

- Strongly enforce existing bans on forced technology transfer that are now part of existing international trade agreements.
- Ban all forced direct and indirect technology transfers in any and all future trade agreements.

Containing China's Space Threat

As chronicled in Chapter 11, "Racing for the Ultimate Strategic High Ground—The Coming China Star Wars," China is ambitiously reaching for the stars even as the U.S. space program continues to stagnate. In fact, America's NASA program has been unable to meet even the least ambitious schedule of Space Shuttle flights. Looming ahead is a significant American "space gap" during which the United States will be *totally incapable* of manned access to space.

America's space gap will occur because the already depleted Space Shuttle fleet will be phased out entirely by around 2010, and the Shuttle's replacement, Orion, is years off and already hitting budget-driven delays. One major casualty of America's looming space gap is likely to be the International Space Station. After the Shuttle is mothballed, the United States won't be able to directly supply or man the station until Orion comes on line—in the best case by 2015 (and likely much later).

Against this backdrop of China rising and a looming American space gap, the United States must

- Reinvigorate the U.S. space program with a vision that simultaneously excites the public imagination, inspires respect in the international community, and produces economically valuable spin-offs and educational benefits.
- Put its money where its space exploration vision is by dramatically increasing NASA's budget. This must be done both to quickly close the coming "space gap" and to avoid America's loss of the ultimate strategic high ground to China.

Finding the required budget dollars for NASA won't be easy in an age of chronic budget deficits and expensive wars. That's why it is critical for every American taxpayer to recognize that space exploration has always "paid for itself." As detailed in Chapter 11, space exploration pays for itself by generating an incredible bounty of new technologies—from GPS and the Internet to solar power, satellite tracking, and medical telemetry.

The problem, of course, with American space economics is that it has typically been the private sector that has reaped most of the benefits of "space spin-offs" while the government and taxpayers have borne most of the costs. This must change in a way that ensures that taxpayers won't have to shoulder the entire NASA burden. One such way to begin to effect such change would be for the United States to:

- Establish a U.S. Space Exploration Commission to identify emerging space-related technologies with large commercial appeal.
- This commission should annually report to Congress on ways to raise revenue from these technologies such as through patenting and licensing.
- Congress should act swiftly on Commission recommendations. This will help defray some of the costs of the space program.

The United States should also seek to build a much stronger public-private partnership with America's growing band of space-related entrepreneurs. Space pioneers such as Paul Allen from Microsoft, Jeff Bezos of Amazon.com, and Elon Musk of PayPal are working overtime to bring the cost of space launch and space travel down to Earth.

For example, Allen's investment of just $20 million with Burt Rutan's Scaled Composites resulted in the world's first private manned space flight. NASA could hardly conduct even a simple design review of a future spacecraft for that price.

Similarly, Musk's lean and mean SpaceX Corporation is ready to launch Air Force payloads at a fraction of the previous cost. In this way, SpaceX is providing NASA with a possible alternative vehicle to plug the coming space gap, and it did so with a mere $278 million grant.

While few in our government or citizenry are aware of the achievements of America's private-sector space program, it's long past time that the U.S. government:

- Adopt policies that acknowledge, support, reward, leverage, and ultimately expand U.S. entrepreneurial space efforts.

In looking at the bigger space picture, it is also essential to recognize that space is about to become a much more crowded place—and not just because of the efforts of China. Other countries, such as Japan, South Korea, India, Iran, and Brazil as well as the European community, are all demonstrating an ambitious new interest and capabilities in space technology. Of course, Russia has long been in the space game, too.

In one scenario, each of these countries will unilaterally reach for the stars in competition with one another and do so in a highly secretive manner. One clear danger from this scenario is the possible weaponization of space by one or more of the countries—with China and Russia being the two countries of most concern. A second very clear danger is space "congestion." Although space is a very big place, the areas in which orbiting Earth satellites can be placed are surprisingly small and already relatively cluttered. Both of these dangers suggest a number of constructive U.S. policy options:

- Partner more closely with the other emerging space-faring nations that share American democratic values and free economic principles. In this way, the United States will gain in relative soft power versus the secretive and authoritarian space powers of China and Russia.
- Push all space exploring nations for verifiable space treaties that prevent the weaponization of space while enlisting the assistance of other nations with an interest in space to make these treaties both practical and enforceable.

- Be prepared to quickly outrace the Chinese (and Russians) if a space arms race cannot be avoided.

What Business Executives Must Do

The world's business executive corps must also stand up and be counted among those who would seek constructive change. As illustrated in Chapter 1, "The Cheating 'China Price' and Weapons of Mass Production," one undeniable major contributor to the world's "Made in China" problem is the ever-increasing propensity of business executives around the world to offshore their factories and production facilities to China—often to evade stronger environmental, health, and safety regulations in the home country.

I always marvel at this lemming-like offshoring behavior because those business executives now falling over each other to open their China beachheads have clearly not thought the problem through. In the parlance of business strategy (which I teach at the business school at the University of California-Irvine), these executives have failed miserably in performing a complete "risk assessment" of moving their facilities to China.

The biggest risk of moving all or most of one's production and research facilities to China that today's business executives are not now properly accounting for is "geopolitical risk." To explain this kind of risk by example, we need only observe that no company executive should want their company held hostage to a trade war with China, a hot war with China, or any one of China's coming "wars from within." Yet what should be very clear from this book is that the likelihood of any one of these types of wars breaking out is rising rapidly.

I might add here parenthetically that when I talk about this issue with corporate executives, I simply ask them this question: Who are we more likely to go to war with, Brazil or China? The answer is self-evident, and within that answer lies this essential truth: Conflicts between China and the rest of the world are only likely to increase as China continues down the path of an unsustainable development driven by unfair trading practices and a rapid destruction of its environment. Although producing in China and selling into the Chinese market may seem very attractive now, when the China problem eventually hits the world fan, the last place your corporation is going to want to be is stuck in China. Accordingly, appropriate strategic recommendations for the world's business executives include

- Don't put all your manufacturing or R&D eggs in one China basket! Companies seeking some type of Asian exposure can diversify into other countries in the region. As the Mattel Corporation painfully learned during the worst product recall in world history, it can be very damaging for any company to have the preponderance of its production in China.
- Play a constructive role in improving China—don't become a lobbyist for Chinese mercantilism just because your company produces in China.
- Understand and harness the growing power and potential profitable opportunities of marketing "Made in the U.S.A" and "Not Made in China" products.
- Significantly increase quality control for those products that your company manufactures and/or distributes from China.

Why America Must Live within Its Means

While China's unfair trading practices constitute the major reason the United States runs huge trade deficits with China, these unfair practices are not the only reason. At least part of America's huge trade imbalance problem may be traced directly to its nearly decade-long descent into a "living beyond one's means" lifestyle. This is a lifestyle that has been accommodated both by chronic federal budget deficits and a surfeit of easy money from the Federal Reserve's "printing press."

America's chronic budget deficits not only overstimulate U.S. demand for Chinese imports. They also require the United States to borrow money from China to finance these budget deficits. This is at least part of the reason that China has become America's de facto "central banker" and why China can now exert undue influence on America's financial and political institutions.

As for the U.S. Federal Reserve, its "easy money" policies have likewise overstimulated import demand for Chinese goods by making it easier for American consumers to use their credit cards to binge on cheap Chinese goods. The Fed's easy money printing press has also indirectly overstimulated the demand for Chinese imports by helping to turn the American home into an ATM.

In particular, during the height of the now-burst housing bubble, artificially low interest rates maintained by the Fed encouraged the "serial refinancing" of many American homes. American homeowners then used equity drawn from their homes in the form of cash loans to boost their consumption, and a big chunk of those ATM dollars flowed offshore to China. From these observations, it follows that

- To help curb its voracious appetite for Chinese imports, the United States must balance its budget, practice monetary restraint, and live within its means.

What China Must (But Probably Won't) Do

If I tell you how things are, I've told you why things cannot change.

—Professor Edward C. Banfield

This sobering observation from one of Harvard's great conservative professors would suggest that there is little or nothing that the Chinese government is going to do to bring about constructive change. I do not, however, entirely share Professor Banfield's "council of despair" on the prospects for internal reform within China. In fact, there are small signs of progress.

For starters, China's latest Five-Year Plan, which was unveiled with great fanfare by President Hu Jintao and Premier Wen Jiabao, marks a significant evolution, if not altogether dramatic shift, from its "Adam Smith on steroids" growth-at-any-cost approach. The centerpiece of this plan is a strong commitment to "sustainable growth" and "balanced development," and it hits many of the right notes.

For example, the plan promises to shift spending priorities away from huge public-works projects such as dam building and water-diversion projects to more bread-and-butter issues such as additional funding for rural health care, better roads and communications networks, safe drinking water, methane facilities to power rural villages, and free compulsory education and textbooks for peasant children. These steps would not only help contain China's own wars from within. They would also have the very welcome collateral effect of building up China's domestic consumption and internal economy and thereby make China much less dependent on selling cheap exports to the world.

China's latest Five-Year Plan also seeks to cut the country's use of energy per unit of economic output by 20% by 2010. More broadly, President Hu has declared that "saving energy and protecting the environment should also be considered a basic state strategy," and he has recommended "the country should promote recycling and the comprehensive use of resources."

To combat rural poverty, the plan seeks to abolish the hated farm taxes, raise farm subsidies, crack down hard on polluters, build more "green buildings," and impose environmental taxes on everything from golf balls and yachts to chopsticks.

On the surface, the chopsticks tax seems comical. It is, however, a serious environmental step. As noted in the *London Independent*:

"The tax on chopsticks will come as a shock to a nation which uses them for breakfast, lunch, and dinner, and where many people have never used a knife and fork. The Chinese use 45 billion pairs of disposable chopsticks every year, which adds up to 1.7 million cubic metres of timber or 25 million fully grown trees."

More broadly, on the international stage, Chinese leaders now routinely promise currency readjustments and the lowering of tariffs and trade barriers. They make repeated big shows about cracking down on piracy and counterfeiting and equally big shows about punishing (and even executing) those who violate food and product safety laws. China's civilian leaders also continue to insist that China comes in peace—its military and nuclear buildups and anti-satellite weapons tests notwithstanding.

On the surface, all of these government commitments, reforms, and public displays would seem to provide cause for at least some optimism. However, the ultimate litmus test question for all of us is this:

- Will China's avowed road to reform truly lead to peace and prosperity or simply wind up as a trail of broken promises, even as China's economic juggernaut continues to spin out of control?

That is a very good question. At this critical juncture, it remains a very much unanswered question. That's precisely why the rest of the world cannot wait for China to get its own house in order. We all must begin to act now.

About the Author

Peter Navarro is a business professor at the University of California-Irvine and author of the bestselling investment book *If It's Raining in Brazil, Buy Starbucks* and the path-breaking management book *The Well-Timed Strategy*.

Professor Navarro is a widely sought-after and gifted public speaker and a regular CNBC contributor. Before joining CNBC, he appeared frequently on Bloomberg TV and radio, CNN, and NPR, as well as on all three major network news shows.

Professor Navarro's unique and internationally recognized expertise lies in his "big picture" application of a highly sophisticated but easily accessible macroeconomic analysis of the business environment and financial markets for consumers, investors, and corporate executives. His articles have appeared in a wide range of publications, from *Business Week*, the *Los Angeles Times*, the *New York Times*, the *Washington Post*, and the *Wall Street Journal* to the *Harvard Business Review*, the *Sloan Management Review,* and the *Journal of Business*.

Professor Navarro's free weekly investment newsletter is published at www.peternavarro.com. His video series, *The China Effect*, appears on YouTube at www.youtube.com/comingchinawars.

Other Books by Peter Navarro

The Well-Timed Strategy: Managing the Business Cycle for Competitive Advantage (2006)

What the Best MBAs Know: How to Apply the Greatest Ideas Taught in the Best Business Schools (2005)

When the Market Moves, Will You Be Ready? How to Profit from Major Market Events (2004)

If It's Raining in Brazil, Buy Starbucks: The Investor's Guide to Profiting from News and Other Market-Moving Events (2001)

The Policy Game: How Special Interests and Ideologues Are Stealing America (1984)

The Dimming of America: The Real Costs of Electric Utility Regulatory Failure (1984)

Acknowledgments

This book benefited greatly from numerous discussions with the many Chinese students in my business school classes at the University of California-Irvine. These students hailed from both the People's Republic of China and the Republic of China (Taiwan). Despite cultural barriers, many were willing to express and share their views candidly in both a classroom setting and private conversations.

I also must offer my sincerest thanks and gratitude to Dr. Cynthia J. Smith, a lecturer in business and anthropology at Ohio State University, and author Russ Hall. Together with my editor Jim Boyd, they all dutifully read numerous drafts of the manuscript and provided constructive editorial and analytical remarks. Of course, any errors and omissions remain my own.

Finally, I would like to thank my very able colleague Greg Autry, who provided much of the inspiration for the chapters on human rights and the Chinese space program—and a considerable amount of the prose.

Peter Navarro
University of California-Irvine
Merage School of Business
www.peternavarro.com

INDEX

FINANCIAL TIMES

In an increasingly competitive world, it is quality
of thinking that gives an edge—an idea that opens new
doors, a technique that solves a problem, or an insight
that simply helps make sense of it all.

We work with leading authors in the various arenas
of business and finance to bring cutting-edge thinking
and best-learning practices to a global market.

It is our goal to create world-class print publications
and electronic products that give readers
knowledge and understanding that can then be
applied, whether studying or at work.

To find out more about our business
products, you can visit us at www.ftpress.com.